RESTING PLACES
in
EAST ANGLIA

Walter Marsden

IAN HENRY PUBLICATIONS

ISBN 0 86025 897 1

First published by
Ian Henry Publications, Ltd.,
20 Park Drive, Romford, Essex RM1 4LH
who would be pleased to hear from readers
making suggestions for inclusions in future editions

Printed in Great Britain by
WBC Print Ltd, Bristol

There are nearly three hundred main entries in this book about people who were buried in East Anglia, and some fifty briefer references. Many of the subjects are celebrities by any reckoning: others are worthies, fortunate or unfortunate. Others again are included because they can 'point a moral or adorn a tale': each, in his or her way, is worth a pilgrimage on an outing or in thought.

One difficulty soon became apparent. People were not always buried in the locality with which they were associated; Rupert Brooke, George Crabbe and Horatio Nelson are almost random examples. Yet they cannot be overlooked and, accordingly, a selection has been included. Sometimes the burial place is unknown, even that of a commanding figure like Boudicca; some of these individuals too are mentioned. Entries in these categories are marked by an asterisk *.

The coverage is by no means exhaustive, partly for reasons of space, partly because no one person can cover the ground. While every care has been taken to ensure accuracy, errors of detail are inevitable, given that the scene changes, more and more particulars become known, 'facts' are modified, even disproved. Publisher and author are at one in hoping that readers will suggest material for inclusion in a future edition and provide up-to-date modifications of information where necessary.

In defining the region there was not much argument about including Norfolk and Suffolk in 'East Anglia'. For the purpose of the book Cambridgeshire has been taken to include Peterborough and the lamented county of Huntingdon. The River Lea is regarded as the western boundary of Essex. I have, very occasionally, disregarded a boundary.

Cambridgeshire

ADAMS, John Couch (1819-92), astronomer, joint discoverer of the planet Neptune. Before taking his degree
at St John's College, Cambridge, Adams decided to
investigate irregularities in the motion of Uranus to
find if they were caused by an unknown, more distant
planet. By October, 1845, he determined the position of
this new planet and sent his findings to the Astronomer
Royal, G B Airy, but did not publish them. In June,
1845, the French astronomer Leverrier, working indepen-
dently, published his calculations, giving a position
within a degree of Adams. Neptune visually discovered
in September, 1846, by Berlin astronomer Galle,
Leverrier being given the major credit, though Adams
was soon acknowledged as co-discoverer. Adams was
appointed Lowndean Professor of Astronomy and Geo-
metry at Cambridge and director of the observatory. He
also furthered research on the November (Leonid)
meteors, the motion of the moon and the earth's
magnetism.
Buried at St Giles Cemetery, Huntingdon Road,
Cambridge, like a number of other notable academics.

ADDENBROOKE, Dr John (1680-1719), founder of
Addenbrooke Hospital, Cambridge. 'A tall thin man
skilled in necromancy': so much is known of him, but
almost nothing about his medical practice. Not much
enthusiasm was aroused by his *Short Essay upon Free-
thinking,* 1714, which advised avoiding prejudice and
using one's powers of thought to the full: 'rather
indefinite', comments *DNB*. Nonetheless, gratefully
remembered for his bequest of £4,500 for a 'small
physical hospital' in Trumpington Street, Cambridge.

Initially having only ten beds, it has long since out-grown the original premises and is a world-famous institution. Addenbrooke was a benefactor of his old college, the red-brick-built St Catherine's, **Cambridge,** where he has a memorial in the chapel.

ALAN of WALSINGHAM (died c.1364), sacrist, then prior of Ely Cathedral from 1341. The Flower of Craftsmen, according to his epitaph, he was outstanding among those who elaborated the Cathedral in the 14th century. Chiefly renowned for his superb rebuilding of the central tower after the Norman tower' collapsed around 1320. Alan's is bigger and octagonal, the most immediately striking feature of the present cathedral. His Octagon is unique in English medieval architecture, for the tower is surmounted by an octagonal lantern and, most impressive, the vault carrying the lantern being too big for Alan to use stone, he daringly used timber. Eight giant oaks, each 63 feet high and three feet thick, now covered with lead, form the corners of the lantern, spanning 70 feet and 152 feet above the floor. It is claimed to be the only Gothic dome in the world.

His other masterpieces include the detached Prior Crauden's Chapel and the Lady Chapel, again with a very wide span, although the stone vaulting is borne on walls that seem half glass: its carvings have been damaged by iconoclasts (See Dowsing, Suffolk).

Inside **Ely** Cathedral, with its hundreds of Norman arches, the painted roofs and other glories, Alan is buried in the north aisle.

Ely, the Island of Eels (some say), rising from the black peat, was where Hereward the Wake held out against William the Conqueror for two years. Apart from the pre-eminent Cathedral, there are the broad, three-storeyed gatehouse called the Porta and other buildings in the precincts, the picturesque Waterside with charming cottages and remarkable Victorian maltings now a public hall for various functions, and the half-timbered house named after Oliver Cromwell,

Balsham Church

who was Governor of the Isle of Ely 1636-47, also known as St Mary's Vicarage or the Steward House.

* ANNA, king of the East Angles (killed 654). Nephew of Raedwald (see Suffolk), father of St Etheldreda of Ely. Put on the throne by the formidable Penda of Mercia, a pagan. Anna was Christian and pious. He had a manor at Exning, near Newmarket, where he lived much of the time. Penda turned against Anna, who fled, but was pursued, defeated and slain. Thought by some until recently that he, not Raedwald, was commemorated at Sutton Hoo. Others identify as his the skeleton recovered from the barrow on **Allington Hill,** east of Cambridge, together with two richly ornamented disks, gilded and set with shell, gold and garnets. One disk in Cambridge Museum, the other in the Ashmolean Museum, Oxford.

BALSHAM, Hugh de (died 1286), bishop of Ely from 1257. Founded Peterhouse, the first Cambridge college. Edward I stayed with him at Balsham, his probable birthplace, near the Fleam Dyke. Buried Ely Cathedral, his heart separately near the altar.

In the large church at Balsham an unusual font cover by a modern rector, Canon Burrell, has figures of Hugh, of Thomas Sutton, founder of Christchurch, and of John de Sleford (died 1401), rector, who built much of the church and who has a big brass, as has John Blodwell (died 1462). Church has elaborately carved 14th century stalls and a medieval rood screen with the rare feature of a loft reached by the old stairs.

BENSON, A[rthur] C[hristopher] (1862-1925), man of letters. Last nighters at the Proms - and practically everybody else - know one thing Benson wrote: the words of *Land of Hope and Glory* to Elgar's *Pomp and Circumstance.* Tall, fair, blue-eyed, comfortably built from middle age, son of Edward White Benson, Archbishop of Canterbury. Sailed through life. Master at Eton. Suggested to an influential friend that, having money, he should become Fellow of Magdalene College,

Cambridge. He did. Better, he became Master of
Magdalene. He wrote. He did a biography of his father,
he contributed to the English Men of Letters series on
Rossetti, Fitzgerald (see Suffolk) and Walter Pater and,
among other writings, he published studies of Tennyson
and Ruskin. Benson was an attractive talker and a
pleasant personality, ready with advice to young writers.
Never married.
Buried St Giles Cemetery, Huntingdon Road, **Cambridge.**

BENTLEY, Richard (1662-1742), classical scholar,
Master of Trinity College, Cambridge. Described as
insufferable, quarrelsome, litigious, arrogant, rapacious,
arbitrary and tactless, his tenure as Master was marked
by violent altercations with the Fellows of Trinity and
with the University, involving lawsuits and intervention
by the government, but Bentley retained his position.
Friend of Sir Isaac Newton, he built an observatory and
organised the University Press as a department of the
University. He gained a European reputation as a
scholar when he exposed the *Letters of Phalaris* as
forgeries. He took part in the controversy of 'Ancients
and Moderns' against Sir William Temple, patron of
Jonathan Swift, who was moved to write *The Battle of
the Books* in 1704. Bentley's children read*The Spectator*
to him, Sir Roger de Coverley affording him much
amusement, and he took Sir Roger's death 'most
seriously to heart'.
Bentley was buried at Trinity College, **Cambridge.**

*BROOKE, Rupert [Chawney] (1887-1915), poet. Lived
at the Old Vicarage, **Grantchester.** His name is on the
village war memorial. Handsome and gifted, Brooke
caugth the imagination of the reading public during the
Great War with poems such as *The Soldier* sonnet: 'If I
should die... a corner of a foreign field that is forever
England' and *The Old Vicarage, Granchester,* written
nostalgically in 1912 as he sat in the Cafe des Westens
on the fashionable Kurfurstendamm in Berlin.
Brooke had travelled to the U S A and the South Seas.
He wrote an enjoyable study *John Webster and the
Elizabethan Drama* (published 1916) and *Democracy and*

the Arts for the Cambridge Fabian Society in 1910 (published 1946).
He died at Skyros on the way to the Dardanelles.
At the bottom of the Old Vicarage garden a Gothic folly was given by Brooke's mother to the father of Peter Ward, who worked alone there, making laboratory equipment, before founding Grant Instruments.
Not only Rupert Brooke, but Chaucer and Byron (his famous Pool), have associations with Grantchester.

BROUGHTON, Urban Huttleston Roger, Baron Fairhaven (1896-1966), sportsman, art collector. Educated in the United States and then at Eton, a Guards officer in the Great War, Broughton combined an interest in horse-racing and other sports with a love of art. He owned the Barton Stud and in 1926, wishing to be near New-market, he bought Anglesey Abbey, an Augustinian foundation of 1135. Here he assembled an art collection (pictures of Windsor Castle, two paintings by Claude, books and many other items) and developed the Abbey grounds into a magnificent garden, all left by him to the National Trust.
Lord Fairhaven was cremated and his ashes were laid in St James's Church, **Lode,** near Anglesey Abbey.
His father, Urban Broughton, died before he could receive the barony intended for him, so it was granted to the son. The village hall at Lode was given as a memorial to Urban Broughton by his widow and child-ren. From the Broughton family the nation received Runnymede meadow, where Magna Carta was sealed.

BROWN, Lancelot 'Capability' (1715-83), landscape gardener. Soon made a name after prentice work at Stowe House, Buckinghamshire. His nickname came not from his own abilities, but from his assessment of an estate as being 'capable' of development. Much in demand as new ideas of improving upon nature spread among the landed gentry. Brown favoured park-like landscapes, depending on form and shape, grass, trees, winding paths and serpentine lakes. His biography, by Dorothy Stroud (Faber, 1975) lists places where Brown did work.

Brown lived in a house on Hall Green, after Fenstanton
-cum-Hilton estate was given to him by the Earl of
Northampton in payment for work at Castle Ashby.
Buried at **Conington,** Huntingdonshire, in what Mee
called a 'rather dingy Gothic revival tomb'. Down one
step from the nave is the large and outstanding
chancel.
*Conington has a lovely village green and an unusual
maze, supposedly very old, cut out of the earth.*

*BURLEY, Sir Simon (1336-88), soldier, courtier, lord
of the manor of Orwell. A friend of Froissart, Burley
fought in France with the Black Prince, who made him
tutor of his son Richard [II]. Burley was promoted by
the young king and negotiated Richard's marriage to
Anne of Bohemia, escorting her to London, for which
mission he was given the Order of the Garter. Later
made Constable of Dover and Warden of the Cinque
Ports. Unfortunately for him, Burley fell foul of the
powerful Earl of Arundel, popular after a naval victory.
Aided by Gloucester, Arundel had Burley arrested and
impeached on various charges. Queen Anne pleaded for
him on her knees after he was condemned, but Arundel
dared to insult her and insisted on the execution.
Burley was beheaded on Tower Hill: his belongings
included a bed 'of green Tarteryn embroidered with
ships and birds'.
At **Orwell** the rector, Anlaby, built the church c.1398
as a memorial to Burley.
*Fine roof with bosses, four of which, bigger than the
rest, are carved with figures still retaining some of the
original colours, thought to represent members of
Burley's family, or, perhaps, Anlaby's.*

BYRTNOTH (slain Maldon 991), Ealdorman of the East
Saxons. Given hospitality by Ely monks, he presented
the Cathedral with several manors (and his daughter
Leoffland left Balsham to Ely) and promised more if
his body was buried there after his death in battle.
Byrtnoth opposed a Danish landing party at Maldon in
991, but allowed the Danes space to fight and they
won, as described in the Old English poem *The Battle of*

Maldon. In it a doomed English warrior says 'Thought shall be the harder/ Heart the keener/ Mood shall be the more/ As our might lessens.' The Danes bore off Byrtnoth's head, but somehow the monks recovered his body and, according to a window in St Mary's Church, Ely, nuns rowed the boat bearing his corpse to **Ely**, where it was buried in what became Bishop West's Chapel in the Cathedral.

CAIUS, John (1510-73), physician, scholar. (Name pronounced. 'Keys' - and sometimes so written). Easy to underestimate, for he was eccentric and credulous: also rich, so by 1557 he could afford to change the status of Gonville Hall, Cambridge, to that of a college, named Gonville and Caius. When he became Master he fell out, as a loyal Roman Catholic, with his Protestant Fellows and had his mass vestments burned.
Caius very early sensed the development of the Renaissance, especially in Italy. After studying theology and - something new - Greek, at Gonville, he went to Italy, worked with Vesalius and took a medical degree at Padua. Back in England he practised medicine so notably that he was nine times President of the College of Physicians and was physician to Edward VI, to Mary and to Elizabeth I.
Caius left his mark on his College by designing gateways for it: the Gate of Humility in the Master's Garden, a second at the entrance to Caius Court, and the Gate of Honour between the Court and the Senate House where degrees are received.
Buried in Caius Chapel, **Cambridge,** with a monument surmounted by a book supporting a skull (modern, 1891) cast from that of Caius.

CATHERINE OF ARAGON (1485-1536), Henry VIII's first queen. Daughter of Ferdinand of Aragon and Isabella of Castille. Said to bear the curse of Deuteronomy on incestuous unions - she was first married to Henry's elder brother, Arthur, Prince of Wales. Of her six children only Mary survived. Henry wanted a male heir and sought annulment of the marriage. The Pope's refusal led to the break with Rome and Wolsey's downfall. Cranmer obtained the divorce. Catherine remained popular, but lived in fear of poison and, indeed, became terminally ill.

Buried in **Peterborough** abbey church, made cathedral by Henry in 1541. Its west front is claimed to be 'the grandest and finest in Europe'. Inside its glories include fan tracery in the retro-choir, the Romanesque nave arcades and the painted nave ceiling. Peterborough monks owned Barnack quarries and used the famous creamy-white stone.

Peterborough was brought prosperity in the 19th century by railways and brickfields and is still developing. Retains Knight's Gateway, Bishop's Palace, west gateway (Norman and 14th century).

Both Catherine and Mary, Queen of Scots, were buried by the verger, Old Scarlett, whose picture is displayed.

CECIL, William, 1st Baron Burghley (1520-98), statesman. 'No prince in Europe had such a councillor', Elizabeth I said of Cecil, her most influential adviser. Cecil began badly by supporting Protector Somerset, but rose through great ability as an administrator under Henry VIII. He reached the heights in Elizabeth's reign: she created him Baron and made him Lord High Treasurer. At home his policy was to curb the Roman Catholics, abroad, to curb Spanish power. His success is embodied in his imposing Elizabethan mansion, Burghley House, with its outstanding facade, roofscapes and gates, not to mention the store of art treasures within, and its park, replanned by Capability Brown, the setting for modern horse trials.

After a funeral service in Westminster Abbey, Burghley's body was transported to a sumptuous tomb of imported marble in **Stamford Baron St Martin's Without**, just south of the River Welland, the Lincolnshire boundary.

Also buried in St Martin's was a bigger man than Lord Burghley. He was Daniel Lambert (1770-1809), 'the heaviest man ever known in England'. Only five feet tall, but weighing 52 stones 11 pounds. His body was 9 feet 4 inches round, his leg 3 feet 1 inch. Lambert was born at Leicester, where he was the keeper of the bridewell, but had to retire because of his enormous weight, though he ate little and drank only water. He had been exhibited in Piccadilly, London, and died suddenly at the Waggon and Horses in St Martin's when passing through Stamford. His walkingstick and a portrait are in the George Hotel and some of his clothes are in the Town Hall.

CLARE, John (1793-1864), 'peasant poet'. 'I am: yet what I am none cares or knows', Clare wrote, summing up his despair after a life dogged by hardship. No money for schooling except what he could earn himself, his childhood poverty at Helpston was relieved by kindly treatment at the Blue Bell Inn. An early gift for verse meant he was taken up briefly by literary folk in London, but Clare was improvident and had to return to Helpston. There he married Patty Turner, not his childhood sweetheart, a farmer's daughter far too grand for him. Then to Northborough in 1832, although he never settled down. From 1832 to 1841 he was treated by humane Dr Matthew Allen at High Beach, Epping Forest, for mental illness. On impulse Clare set off penniless for Northborough, walking 80 miles in three days. Trouble still haunted him and presently he was forcibly committed to Northampton General Lunatic Asylum, found guilty of 'years addicted to poetical prosings' and spent his last 22 years there. Clare's merits as a poet have long been recognised. His verse is marked by favourite reading, ballads and the Bible, and by close observation of nature, deriving from his interest in wild life, especially birds and plants (which he collected on long rambles as a young man). Antiquities also fascinated Clare.
Buried in **Helpston** churchyard, its church given a very individual look by the short spike of a spire abruptly rising from a somewhat dumpy tower. Memorial to Clare near the Helpston Cross (c.1330). Some relics of his are in the Priestgate Museum, Peterborough.

CLAYPOLE, John, see CROMWELL, Elizabeth

CLOUGH, Anne Jemima (1820-92), first principal of Newnham College, Cambridge. Sister of the poet Arthur Hugh Clough, Anne wanted to write, but went into teaching and became interested in higher education for

women. In 1870 Henry Sedgwick proposed lectures in Cambridge for women and presently a house of residence was established for those who came long distances to attend, with Miss Clough as Head. Five students were housed in Regent Street. More and more women students came and a new house, Newnham Hall, was built, thanks to £10,000 subscribed by supporters. This was the old hall of the present College, which was opened in 1880. Though not a great organiser, Miss Clough had a strong personality, showed much integrity and was popular with students.
Buried in **Grantchester** churchyard. The glorious bronze gates at Newnham are her memorial.

COLE, Rev. William (1714-82), antiquary. As a boy Cole copied inscriptions and drew coats of arms. At Eton with Horace Walpole, who noted Cole's Roman Catholic tendencies.Cole was well off and thus able to collect manuscripts, many of them on continental travels. He had acquired a fine collection by 1765, when he was in France with Walpole, who dissuaded him from turning Catholic and settling in that country, arguing that, if he did so, the King of France would have the power to take Cole's manuscripts. Returned to Cambridgeshire, where at Waterbourn he was much discomforted by floods, by gout and by zealots of several denominations. He moved to Milton, near Cambridge, becoming known as Cole of Milton or Cardinal Cole. He published no work, but helped many students and scholars. After much hesitation Cole left nearly a hundred folio-sized volumes of manuscripts in his own handwriting to the British Museum.
Cole bequeathed money for erecting the steeple of St Clement's, **Cambridge,** under which he is buried. Not everyone admires his steeple!

COOK (née Batts), Elizabeth (1740-1835), wife of Captain James Cook. They married at Barking in 1762 and she survived her great navigator husband by 56 years, outlived her children and was alone for the last forty years of her life. She last saw Captain Cook as he set off for his third and fatal voyage: it was twenty

months after his death in Hawaii in 1779 before she knew of it.
Monument to Captain Cook, his wife and their six children (she and two children buried in church) in St Andrew's the Great, **Cambridge,** a redoubtable stronghold of Puritanism in Elizabethan and Stuart times.

COTTON, Sir Robert Bruce (1571-1631), antiquary and book collector. His pursuits gained him a European reputation and a wide circle of friends from Ben Jonson, Bacon and Raleigh to William Camden, with whom he founded the Society of Antiquaries. James I thought much of him and made him a baronet. Success brought enemies; he was imprisoned in 1615 accused of trying to shield the Earl of Somerset. Cotton turned against Charles I and was framed, escaping prison by amnesty on birth of the future Charles II in 1630. His great library was sealed and, deprived of it, he pined away. Cotton gave some of his manuscripts to Sir Thomas Bodley for Oxford University Library and the remainder eventually went to the British Museum (the Cottonian MS).
James I called Cotton 'cousin' from his descent from the Bruce. Cotton was responsible for the many monuments to his ancestors in **Conington** church, where he is buried. One, erected in 1600, is to King David I of Scotland (Earl of Huntingdon) and his son, Henry of Scotland. Late in the 17th century the great woodcarver Grinling Gibbons signed his carved head of Robert Cotton, aged 14. The spire of the church, a landmark, leans somewhat to the west. This is not, of course, the Conington where Capability Brown was buried.

CROMWELL (nee Bourchier), Elizabeth (1598-1665), wife of Oliver Cromwell. After Cromwell's death his widow was allowed to retire to Northborough, where the Claypole (sometimes Claypoole, see Essex) family lived. Cromwell's second daughter, also Elizabeth, his favourite child, married John Claypole in 1646. He became Cromwell's Master of Horse. The daughter died in 1658 and was buried in Westminster Abbey, but John survived until 1688, although imprisoned for a time.

Mrs Cromwell and John Claypole were buried in St Andrew's, **Northborough,** a small church without a tower. Mrs Cromwell's grave is believed to be under a large stone, which has had to be repaired, in the floor. A tablet to her is on the east wall, from the Cromwell Association.
John Clare's wife, Martha (Patty, née Turner) was buried in the churchyard.

CROMWELL, Henry (1628-74), Lord-Lieutenant of Ireland, 'the best of Cromwell's sons' (Carlyle). After the Restoration Henry Cromwell farmed at the Spinney, Wicken. Charles II once visited him from Newmarket and a courtier paraded with a pitchfork before Cromwell, a reference to his having been mace-bearer in Ireland when Cromwell was Lord-Lieutenant. The King, however, was not amused.
Henry Cromwell is buried in **Wicken** church. So, too, Oliver's sister, Elizabeth (died 1672) and the Protector's grandson, Oliver (died 1658).
James Wentworth Day, author of A history of the Fens and many other works, lived in the village.
Wicken Fen of 700 acres, managed by the National Trust, is a much-studied nature reserve, the oldest in Britain. A unique draining mill has been restored. Visitors' centre, angling facilities, hide for bird-watchers.

CROMWELL, Oliver (1599-1658), Lord Protector, 'God's Englishman'. In her *Cromwell: our chief of men,* Lady Antonia Fraser tells of Cromwell's head's adventures after the Protector's body was dug up in 1661, hung at Tyburn, decapitated and buried at the foot of the gallows. The head itself remained stuck on a pole on Westminster Hall for many years, then blown down, retrieved by a sentinel and sold to a Cambridgeshire family. It was acquired by the proprietor of a London museum, who sold it to three people, one a woman, for £230 for exhibition about the time of the French revolution. The woman gave it to her doctor, Dr Josiah Henry Wilkinson of Shortlands, Kent. It descended through the family to Canon Horace Wilkinson of Woodbridge, Suffolk, who arranged for decent burial in

1960 near the chapel of Cromwell's old college, Sidney Sussex, **Cambridge.** Size six and seven eighths, depression for wart over eye. Trepanned after death for embalming.

D'AYE, Mrs Elizabeth, Oliver Cromwell's great-granddaughter. This story of three Elizabeths begins badly and does not improve in the next generation, but ends happily. It starts with the Protector's son, Henry, whose only grown-up daughter Elizabeth married William Russell, an army officer who ran into debt and died owing money. Mrs Russell's daughter, Elizabeth, seemed to be set for happiness, marrying a rich man from Soham, Robert D'Aye. Unfortunately D'Aye was a spendthrift, went through all his money and ended in the workhouse. Mrs D'Aye died practically penniless: she, too, had a daughter Elizabeth and it was she who stopped the rot, through not pitching her sights too high. This third Elizabeth might have thought herself lucky, bearing in mind her parents' latter circumstances, to marry the Soham shoemaker. He turned out to be a steady character and improved his situation, supposedly rising to be high-constable.
To get back to Mrs D'Aye, she was buried in the grave yard of St Andrew's, **Soham.** The church of flint flushwork has a grand tower topped with battlements and pinnacles, while the nave is distinguished by its lovely roof.
The churchyard was made above a pagan East Anglian cemetery. Like Ely, Soham is on an island among the fens. The place, large by fenland standards, has been modernised and given a village college and recreational facilities.
St Felix of Burgundy, first Bishop of East Anglia, founded a monastery at Soham and was buried there 647. His remains were removed to Ramsey in the 11th century. It is said that on Soham Mere (since drained) the monks of Ely and Ramsey had a boat race, the winners to take St Felix's remains.

DOWNING, Sir George (1623-84), politician. Built houses, including what are now Nos. 10 and 11, on land he leased in what is now Downing Street. Downing's family emigrated to America (his mother was sister of John Winthrop, Governor of Massachusetts) and Downing studied and later taught at the recently-founded Harvard University. He returned to England in 1645 and swiftly rose under the Commonwealth to be Ambassador to France, then to Holland, but he betrayed secrets to Royalists, thereby gaining great wealth. Later Charles II gave him offices of much profit. Downing lured three Commonwealth exiles into a trap - one had greatly helped him earlier - and arranged for their repatriation for execution. He remained avaricious and ungenerous; his mother had complained of his stinginess to her, wealthy though he was. 'A most ungrateful villain', Pepys said of Downing.

He is buried at **Croydon:** a simple church on a hill among trees. The interior is unspoiled despite some re-building in 1685. There is a fireplace in the squire's pew.

DOWNING, Sir George (1684-1749), grandson of above. His will was much disputed for fifty years by Cam-bridge University and the widow of the childless last heir, Sir Jacob Downing (d.1764), when the widow should have parted with money intended for founding a new College. At last, in 1800, money was made available to found the elegant, Greek-style Downing College, Cambridge, designed by William Wilkins.

Downing married at 15 a girl of 13; they parted on completion of the ceremony, though the marriage was not annulled. Downing's was 'a most miserable, covetous and sordid existence'.

Downing buried, like his grandfather, at **Croydon.**

EDDINGTON, Sir Arthur Stanley (1882-1944), astro-physicist. Called the modern Archimedes. From 1916 studied the constitution and evolution of stars. Early interested in Einstein's theory of generalised relativity, doing much by his work and advocacy to ensure its acceptance. Director of the ·Cambridge Observatory from 1914, Eddington kept up a remarkable flow of studies ranging from cosmological to atomic. Plumian

Ely Cathedral

Professor of Astronomy and Experimental Philosophy at Cambridge. Also interested in mathematics and the philosophy of science. Author of several popular books, including *The Expanding Universe*, 1933. His achievements were recognised in his lifetime; made a Fellow of the Royal Society, 1914 (its Royal Medal in 1928); knighted 1930; given Order of Merit 1938.
Buried St Giles Cemetery, **Cambridge.**

ELYOT, Sir Thomas (c.1490-1546), scholar, author and diplomat. Said to have introduced the words 'aristocracy', 'democracy', 'society' and 'liberty' in his Humanist work *The Boke named the Governour*, 1531, intended for the education of princes. In addition Elyot made translations, compiled anthologies and wrote learned books and original works. Friend of Roger Ascham and Sir Thomas More. Sent against his will on embassy to Emperor Charles V to secure approval of Catherine of Aragon's divorce, Elyot was told by the Emperor at Naples that More had been executed. Involved in the reception of Henry VIII's unwanted Anne of Cleves. Played a part in the proceedings for the arrest of William Tyndale.
Buried **Carlton-cum-Willingham,** a small church in a pleasantly wooded setting. Two medieval bells in the reconstructed bellcote.

*ETHELDREDA, Saint (c.630-679), founder of Ely monastery. Daughter of King Anna. First married to Tonbert, a noble, from whom he received the Isle of Ely as a marriage gift. Soon widowed and always devout, she entrusted her estate to her steward Ovin (commemorated by broken, inscribed shaft in the nave of Ely Cathedral). Etheldreda was later persuaded to marry Ecfrith, King of Northumberland, but left him for a holy life; he pursued her, but a flood foiled him. Remembering Tonbert's gift, Etheldreda went to Ely and founded a monastery in 673, succeeded by the cathedral.
Also known as St Audrey or Awdrey, patroness of a fair notorious for gimcrack wares, hence our term 'tawdry'.

Etheldreda buried Ely Cathedral, but her remains lost, because the building was destroyed by Danes, though, of course, rebuilt as the present magnificent edifice. Her left hand, the one surviving relic, is in a shrine in St Etheldreda's Roman Catholic Church, Ely. Etheldreda had three sisters (see Wythburga [Norfolk]).

FAWCETT, Henry (1833-84), economist and statesman. Blind at 25 from a shooting accident, Fawcett spoke for all the visually handicapped when he asked that they should not be patronised, should be treated without special reference to their misfortune and, especially, helped to be independent. He kept up long walks, skating, angling and horse-riding. Became a Fellow of Trinity Hall, Cambridge, and later Professor of Economics. Author of several books, elected Liberal MP and made Postmaster-General by Gladstone.
Fawcett married Millicent Garrett (1847-1929), sister of Elizabeth Garrett Anderson and leader of the constitutional movement for women's suffrage; she opposed militant Emmeline Pankhurst. Dame Millicent also campaigned for university reform and was involved in the foundation of Newnham College.
Henry Fawcett buried in the churchyard at Trumpington, whose church has a famous brass effigy made for Sir Giles Trumpington, a crusader with the future Edward I; Sir Giles survived his son, Sir Roger II, and altered the brass, a cross-legged effigy with trumpets on the shield, for him.

FECKENHAM, John (died 1584), last Abbot of Westminster. He found the Confessor's coffin during his restoration of the Abbey. A fervent Catholic, but no persecutor of Protestants under Mary Tudor. Attended Lady Jane Grey on the scaffold after humbly declining to attempt her conversion. Befriended the future Elizabeth I, so not at first molested even though he had preached Mary's funeral sermon. Remained true to his faith, so at last dismissed, penalised and sent to the Tower for a time. Eventually imprisoned in Wisbech Castle; unknown grave in Wisbech churchyard.
Among Wisbech's many features, the Nene's curve is

followed by two rows of Georgian houses. In one, the South Brink, Octavia Hill, co-founder of the National Trust and pioneer of housing reform, was born in 1838. In North Brink the outstanding Peckover House (National Trust). In graveyard in its grounds there is a stone marked 'J S 88 1742', said to be that of Jane   Stuart, natural daughter of James II. After he fled his throne, she came to Wisbech and offered herself as a servant at the hiring by the bridge; later turned Quaker. Wisbech has a monument to Thomas Clarkson,   the abolitionist, who was born there (see Suffolk).

FERRAR, Nicholas (1592-1637), contemplative. Active enough for much of his life: Ferrar studied medicine at Cambridge, travelled for several years on the continent, for a while with the suite of Charles I's sister Elizabeth. Returning, Ferrar acted as King's Counsel, then became Deputy Governor of the Virginia Company. MP for Lymington, Hampshire, 1624. A great change came over him after he took Holy Orders. He retired to Little Gidding with his family in 1626 and founded a religious community which inspired J H Shorthouse's *John Inglesant* and the last of T S Eliot's *Four Quartets*. The community practised various crafts under the instruction of tutors employed by Ferrar and published several religious books, two of them made specially for Charles I, who visited Little Gidding in 1633.
Ferrar thought to be buried at **Little Gidding:** damaged table tomb outside the door of the church said to be his. Tiny church rebuilt in brick in Classical style.

FEW, Jabez (died 1920s), white witch, of Willingham. See Murrell, Suffolk.

HOBSON, Thomas (c.1544-1631), carrier. 'Hobson's Choice' was originally 'take the horse by the stable door [the longest rested] or none'. Very successful, became rich. Puritan mayor of Cambridge. Largely responsible for bringing the city a supply of water for drinking and sanitation. Runnels along the sides of Trumpington and St Andrew's Streets still exist. College ponds and swimming pools still supplied by Hobson's

Conduit, an octagon under a dome, topped by a golden pineapple.
Hobson buried near Thomas Fuller, church historian and antiquarian, at St Benet's Church, **Cambridge,** to which he gave a Bible and other books (displayed).
In St Benet's Saxon tower change-ringing was intro-
duced in the 17th century by Fabian Steadman, clerk to
the parish. A printer, Steadman gave the bellringers
slips of paper with the changes printed on them.

HOLCROFT, Francis (c.1629-93), Puritan minister. Fellow of Clare Hall, Cambridge. Ejected from Bassing-bourne 1662, seized while preaching, tried and condemned to banishment, but allowed to remain in the country through Lord Anglesey's intercession - only to be imprisoned as an insolvent debtor at Cambridge and in the Fleet. Nevertheless Holcroft resumed preaching after James II fled.
It used to be held that Holcroft was buried at Triplow, but more recently considered that his grave is at **Oakington,** with those of Joseph Oddy and Henry Osland, who were also ejected for preaching Puritanism.
Oakington church fitted with red warning lights for
low-flying aircraft from RAF base.

HOLLAND, Sir Sydney George, 3rd baronet and 2nd Viscount Knutsford (1855-1931), hospital administrator and reformer. Known admiringly, if unofficially, as the Prince of Beggars for his work in raising more than £5 million over 30 years for London Hospital, as its chairman. Before that a dedicated worker as chairman of Poplar Hospital, 1891-6. Influential in improving hospital administration and nursing.
Buried **Bassingbourn** churchyard, at his request without any wreath on coffin or funeral oration.
Church has tiny spire on tower; inside, Nightingale
family monuments and collection of theological books
given by Sir Edward Nightingale in 1717; also early
Tudor churchwardens' accounts. Village college.

HUDDLESTON, John, 'once Chamberlayne unto Kinge Phylipe and Captaine of his Garde, and one of Queen

Maryes most honourable Privie Counsel'. Thus his inscription at **Sawston,** but it omits what Huddleston is best remembered for - his sheltering of Mary Tudor a few days before she was proclaimed Queen. It was a near shave, for Mary had to disguise herself as a market woman to get away. In revenge Lady Jane Grey's supporters ordered Sawston Hall to be burned. Mary, however, gave Huddleston permission to use stone from Cambridge Castle for a new house.

LAW, William (1686-1761), Anglican divine and writer. The enjoyable qualities of Law's writing would be difficult to anticipate from his life-style. Declined the oath of allegiance to George I, so forfeiting his Fellow-ship of Emmanuel College, Cambridge. Tutor to Edward Gibbon's father, 1727-37, Law retired to his birthplace, Kingscliffe, near Stamford, in 1740. His pupil's sister came as a disciple, as did a widow, joining in good works and a life ruled by prayer. Law got up very early, went very early to bed, existing on very little, though not lacking money. His generosity attracted beggars to the consternation of his neighbours. His writings were very influential; Dr Johnson first turned to religion after reading Law's *A Serious Call to a Devout and Holy Life,* published 1729, and John Wesley derived much of his teaching from Law. His work is anything but dull. He could be caustic when exposing stupidity, could rarely resist an epigram - even when it interfered with the spiritual message - capable of incisive logic, a master of terse and vigorous English and ever ready to display his brilliant wit. Buried **Kingscliffe.**

LITTLEPORT RIOTERS of 1816 (William Beames, George Crow, John Dennis, Isaac Hartley, Thomas South: all hanged). Farm workers and Napoleonic Wars veterans provoked by high food prices and unemployment - and the callousness of the parish officer, a rich farmer Henry Martin, who flaunted his expensive clothes and said that the parish allowance was ample - demon-strated and rioted from Littleport to Ely before the military rounded them up. Twenty-four, one a woman,

condemned to death, but 19 reprieved and transported to Botany Bay. Great local sympathy. The butcher who supplied the cart to take the five to the gallows was later found head down in his own cess pit. The corpse of the carpenter who made their coffins was discovered in the pipe taking water to Ely brewery.
The five hanged were buried in one grave at **Ely**. Memorial tablet on the tower of St Mary's, Ely. Church has good north door, unusual nave arcades (semi-arched) and flat panelled ceiling. Also memorial window to Byrtnoth.

LUMPKIN, Captain Anthony (died 1780). The Lumpkins of Leverington counted Oliver Goldsmith as a family friend and claimed that he came to stay with them. While he was there he is thought to have written part of his stage comedy *She Stoops to Conquer*,   1773, while sitting under the village mulberry tree. It is also said that Goldsmith took the Captain's name for the character Tony Lumpkin of the play. None of this is confirmed in John Ginger's 1977 biography of Goldsmith, *The Notable Man*.
Captain Anthony has a wall monument in **Leverington** church, notable for its lofty tower and spire and, inside, the glass on a perpendicular font.

*MALLORY, George Leigh (1886-1924), mountaineer. Last seen with A C Irvine only 800 feet below the summit of Everest, which he wanted to climb 'because', he said, 'it is there'. Attracted to climbing from boyhood, he taught at Charterhouse. He worked at Cambridge for the Board of Extra-Mural Studies. His first expedition to the Himalayas was in 1921. Bad weather dogged his last climb.
Magdalene, Mallory's old **Cambridge** College, named a new court after him. Plaque over doorway.

*MARY, Queen of Scots (1542-87). Nearly Queen of England - if only the Scots had agreed to her marriage to the future Edward VI; nearly Queen of France - but her husband, the Dauphin, died 18 months after the wedding. Queen at last, but had to abdicate. Married the Earl of Darnley, her cousin and great-grandson of

Henry VII, who murdered her Italian favourite, David Rizzio, then was murdered by the Earl of Bothwell, soon Mary's husband. Scots nobles forced her to flee to England and seek her cousin, Elizabeth's, support. Instead Elizabeth imprisoned her. Mary Stuart's romantic and tragic life ended on the block at Fotheringay.
Buried in **Peterborough** Cathedral, as was Catherine of Aragon. The library has a letter from James I ordering the removal of his mother's remains to Westminster Abbey in 1612.

MAY, Sir Thomas Erskine, 1st Baron Farnborough (1815-86), constitutional jurist. Son of an attorney in Kentish Town, May was unable for financial reasons to take up an exhibition to Oxford and had to accept the first job available. This was on the staff of the House of Commons. He served there all his life: assistant librarian, 1831; clerk to the Commons, 1871-81; then given peerage. Standard work on the *Constitutional History of England... 1760-1860,* but best known for the MPs' 'book of rules', his authoritative *Practical Treatise on the Law, Privileges, Proceedings and Usage of Parliament,* marked by 'profound, accurate and well-digested learning' (*DNB*). Translated into various languages. 'Erskine May' has joined the ranks of works like Baedeker and Debrett, their name a byword. Erskine May was so respected that once, during his last illness, the chimes of Big Ben were silenced by order of the Speaker and tan was spread in the courtyard to muffle the noise of carriage wheels.
Buried **Chippenham**, near the church's 15th century porch, notable for two formidable gargoyles.
Brick school of 1714 and picturesque cottages near church. Chippenham Fen is a nature reserve.

MONTAGU, John, 3rd earl of Sandwich (1718-92), politician. His title is known at home and abroad, for he invented the sandwich. An inveterate gambler, he resented having to stop for meals, so he avoided interruption by eating some meat between two pieces of bread. His title was also given to the Sandwich Islands in the Pacific and the South Sandwich Islands in the Antarctic Ocean. Montagu has been described as one of the worst First Lords of the Admiralty (see Keppel, Suffolk).

Montagu buried in family vault at **Kimbolton,** the place where Catherine of Aragon died after being moved to the Castle from Buckden.

Vanbrugh is said to have redesigned Kimbolton Castle in the much-praised town.

*The Pepys family was related to the Montagus. The career of Samuel Pepys, the diarist, later Secretary to the Admiralty, was aided by Edward Montagu, 1st earl of Sandwich, drowned at the Battle of Sole Bay, South-wold, 1672 (see Haddock, Essex). Pepys' parents lived at Brampton and it was there that he buried his diary during Dutch invasion scares. In **Brampton** church, which has a 14th century screen and stalls and a fine 15th century roof, a memorial to Pepys' sister Paulina (Mrs Jackson), 'last of ye family of ye Peps in this parish 1689'. Another memorial at Brampton to Lady Olivia Bernard Sparrow, 19th century Anglican evangelist and philanthropist, who rebuilt houses in a very individualistic style, marked 'O.B.S.' on walls, for some of her tenants, to whom she relentlessly 'did good', and an octagonal house with cottage and courtyard in the High Street.*

NORTH, Dudley, 3rd baron North (1581-1666), courtier. In 1606 North discovered the benefits of the waters of what became Royal Tunbridge Wells and also publicised the waters of Epsom. Aloof from the Civil War. A French scholar who wrote essays and poems. Musical: composed and sang songs, and played the treble viol. Fond of family musical picnics at Kirtling in a glade he called Tempe.

Buried **Kirtling** in the Norths' chapel, effigy in black armour tipped with gold. Other members of the family buried there: Edward North, 1st baron North (1496-1564), built the brick chapel and also Kirtling Towers, of which only the turreted gatehouse survives; 2nd baron, Roger (1530-1600), a friend of Leicester, distinguishing himself at Zutphen and entertaining

Elizabeth I at Kirtling in 1578: he has a slate six-poster tomb. 4th baron also buried there in 1677; he had 14 children, one of whom, Roger, wrote *The Lives of the Norths.*

OLEY, Rev. Barnabas (1602-86), Royalist divine. Vicar of Great Gransden from 1635. During the Civil War he collected and smuggled Cambridge University plate by devious routes to Charles I at Nottingham (1642) to raise money. Oley himself lent money on valuable gold communion plate of Clare, his college, and restored it in 1660. He paid dearly for his partisanship, losing his fellowship in 1644, his possessions and property and his benefice. He spent seven years wandering England in poverty, but his fortunes were restored under Charles II. He edited George Herbert's poems in 1652 - they had been fellow students.

Oley built the vicarage at **Great Gransden,** a better job than the 15th century rebuilding of the church, where Oley has a tablet. Tower and nave, chancel and nave, out of alignment, chancel arch somewhat askew, suggesting replacement piecemeal. Oley made several gifts to the church, among them six leather fire-buckets.

PATEMAN, Elizabeth (murdered 1734). The story goes that in 1734 a chapman came to Steeple Morden and stayed overnight at Moco Farm (now demolished) on Cheyney Water. He was never seen again. The villagers suspected the farmer of murder as he suddenly stopped using his well and filled it in. The farmer and his wife are said to have overheard their servant, Elizabeth Pateman, tell her sweetheart that she had a secret to reveal to him the next time they met. Apparently fearing they would be betrayed, they murdered her with a billhook, a knife and a ploughshare. The chapman's disappearance was never explained, nor were the farmer or his wife found guilty of either murder.

Elizabeth is buried in **Steeple Morden** churchyard under a stone carved with the implements traditionally held to have killed her.

PEPYS - see Montagu.

PERSE, Dr Stephen (1548-1615), founder of Perse
Grammar School in Cambridge. A physician who became
wealthy and acquired property in Cambridge. A Fellow
of Gonville and Caius College from 1571, bursar 1570
and 1592. Founded six fellowships and six scholarships
at Caius: founded almshouses, since rebuilt, now in
Newnham. He provided a 'sufficient Causey', a raised
path between Jesus Lane and Barnwell. Most of his
property went towards establishing a free grammar
school, which moved to Hills Road in 1888: the old
building (bought by the University) had a fine Jacobean
roof which was preserved and bought to Hills Road in
1960.
Perse monument (kneeling effigy) in chapel of Caius
College, **Cambridge.**

PORSON, Richard (1759-1808), Greek scholar. Porson
could stand as the model for the eccentric professor:
slovenly, often procrastinatory and indolent, given to
drinking bouts, a greedy eater, yet kind to friends and
helpful to strangers. Son of a Norfolk weaver, Porson
showed such promise so early that the local curate
educated him with his own sons, then the squire had
him sent to Eton in 1774. Friends enabled him to enter
Trinity College, Cambridge, where he soon became
scholar and fellow. At 33 he was Regius Professor of
Greek. Refusing to take orders cost him his scholarship.
Became known in learned circles for textual criticism,
for instance defending Gibbon's rejection of the episode
of the three heavenly witnesses in St John, chapter V
as an interpolation. Porson wrote serious papers, but
also light essays; a strong Whig, he contributed to the
Morning Chronicle. In his main field he scrutinised
Greek metre, edited four plays of Euripides and
prepared an edition of Aeschylus. His Greek calligraphy
was exquisite.
He is buried in the chapel of Trinity College,
Cambridge.

SAUNDERSON, Nicholas (1682-1739), mathematics
scholar. Childhood smallpox blinded him, but Saunderson
was so gifted that he learned classics at school and, by

25, was teaching mathematics at Cambridge. Praised by Lord Chesterfield, and made doctor of law. Like many blind people he had acute hearing; he sensed the size of a room by the sound of his voice and used echo from wall to wall to gauge his whereabouts. Similarly, his sense of touch was so highly developed that he could allegedly detect false medals by fingering them.

Buried **Bottisham,** a fenland village with one of the county's best churches, containing monuments to Jenyns family, one of whom survived the Valley of Death at Balaclava. Also bust of Saunderson beside the Bath in Christ Church Fellows' Garden, **Cambridge,** with Milton and Platonist Cudworth; nearby is an urn to C[harles] P[erry] (Lord) Snow, whose novel, *The Masters,* is about Christ's. The Bath is supplied by water from Hobson's Conduit.

SMITH, Sir Harry George Wakelyn (1787-1860), soldier and administrator. Serving in the Peninsular War, Smith befriended a Spanish girl who became his wife, as told in Georgette Heyer's *The Spanish Bride.* Smith fought at Waterloo and led the victorious charge against the Sikhs at Aliwal in 1846. Governor of the Cape of Good Hope; commemorated in names of South African towns Harrismith, Ladysmith, Whittlesea and Aliwal.

Buried **Whittlesea** cemetery with his wife. Community College named after him. There is an 1862 marble monument and bust in St Mary's Church; chancel aisle called 'Sir Harry's Chapel'.

St Mary's tower and crocketed spire 'one of the sights of England' (Shell guide). 17th century Butter Cross in Market Place. Many local brickworks chimneys. John Clare came looking for plants around his admired Whittlesea Mere, now drained.

TABOR (or TALBOR), Sir Robert (1642-81), physician. Experiments with quinine ('Jesuits' bark') in Essex marshland convinced Tabor that it should be given oftener and in smaller quantities than thitherto. Said to have cured Charles II's fever, thereupon being appointed a royal physician in ordinary. Went to France and restored the Dauphin by 'the Englishman's cure'. Tabor declined Louis XIV's invitation to stay in France, but is said to have sold him the secret of his treatment. Tabor also cured the Queen of Spain. Wall monument to Tabor in Holy Trinity Church, **Cambridge,** later the centre of the Cambridge evangelical revival.

TYE, Dr Christopher (c.1500-73), church composer. Wrote the tune 'While shepherds watched their flocks by night.' The story goes that when Elizabeth I criticised his playing, Tye retorted that her ears were out of tune. To receive his Mus.Doc. degree Tye had to wear a doctor of medicine's robes, since musical graduates then had no distinctive robes. His compositions were almost entirely sacred: masses in Henry VIII's reign, Protestant hymns in Edward VI's. He was music master in Mary's reign and, perhaps, organist to Elizabeth. It may be that through Tye polyphonic music was kept from extinction in post-Reformation England. He left much work unpublished. Tye was for long at Ely, where he took deacon's orders in 1560 and was ordained priest. He held the living at Little Wilbraham in the 1560s.
Tye retired to **Doddington-cum-Marsh** and is supposed to be buried there.
Doddington long claimed to be the county's biggest parish, its rectory the wealthiest in England. The church is near the main road; angels in the roof of the largely-restored nave, window designed by William Morris.

VASSA, Anna Maria (1793-97). 'Daughter of Vassa the African', a rescued slave: so much and, tantalisingly, no more is known from a wall tablet in St Andrew's Church, **Chesterton.**
The church (not the new one) has a beautiful 14th century spire and carved benches. The county jail and assize courts are in Chesterton, almost a suburb of Cambridge. Bumping races and other events on the Cam hereabouts.

WASHINGTON, Rev. Godfrey (died 1729), great-uncle of

George Washington. Vicar of St Mary the Less, Cambridge, 1705-29. The iconoclast William Dowsing (see Suffolk) smashed sixty 'superstitious pictures, some Popes and Crucifixes and God and Father sitting in a chayer and holding a Glasse in his hand'. Church built as St Peter's in the 12th century, renamed after rebuilding in the 14th century, still connected by gallery to Peterhouse.

Washington is buried in St Mary the Less, **Cambridge.** American visitors are intrigued by the design over his monument, much resembling the Stars and Stripes and the eagle of freedom.

WATERHOUSE, Rev. Joshua (died 1827), eccentric. His will directed that he should be buried 18 feet down beside his favourite horse. He wasn't. His behaviour so upset his servant Joshua Slade that he murdered his master and put the body in a bran tub. Slade caught hiding in a culvert and hanged at Huntingdon. Waterhouse got a table tomb near the entrance to – **Little Stukely** church, at the top of the ascending main street.

Big Alconbury airfield nearby.

WEST, Nicholas (1461-1533), bishop of Ely and diplomatist. His brillant success on many missions abroad enabled West to live luxuriously, attended by 100 servants. He provided food daily for 200 poor people and gave money to offset high corn prices. Among his triumphs was a commercial treaty with the Netherlands in 1506. Henry VIII appointed him dean of St George's, Windsor, where West completed St George's Chapel. After more commissions he treated with Louis XII of France, who married Henry's sister, Mary, and with Francis I, who succeeded Louis. For this West was made bishop of Ely in 1515. There he reformed the administration. He later negotiated with Francis I to obtain compensation for Wolsey for resigning the bishopric of Tournai.

West built part of the provost's lodging at King's, his Cambridge college. Better known for his Chapel in **Ely** Cathedral, where he is buried: interesting for early use of Renaissance motifs.

WILKINS, William (1778-1839), architect. Born Norwich, his father an architect and antiquarian. Wilkins studied at Caius College, Cambridge. In 1801 he toured Greece, Asia Minor and Italy. His 1804 design for Downing College shows strong Classical Greek influence. Wilkins designed Haileybury College for the East India Company in 1806, worked on the spire of Yarmouth church in 1807 and designed the Nelson Column at Gorleston in 1817. After much work in Cambridge (for example, King's College, Trinity and Corpus Christi) Wilkins designed University College, London, St George's Hospital, London, and the National Gallery (his scope much restricted and his designs later altered). Wilkins died in **Cambridge** and was buried in the chapel of Corpus Christi, which he had erected.

WITTGENSTEIN, Ludwig Josef Johann (1889-1951), mathematician and philosopher. As a man daunting, aloof, austere, a harsh judge of others: as a philosopher second only to Bertrand Russell in this century, according to A J Ayer in his 1985 study. Born in Vienna, Wittgenstein lived much in England. He had inherited considerable wealth from his father, but gave it away, not to the poor, whom it might corrupt, but to relatives already so rich it couldn't harm them. During World War II Wittgenstein worked as a medical orderly in Guy's Hospital, unrecognised as a Cambridge professor. Whereas most modern philosophers concentrated on the theory of knowledge, Wittgenstein turned to the study of meaning and, hence, of language. He accepted the importance of language as a tool of scientific analysis, but was mistrustful of the prestige of science. Since argument continues over Wittgenstein's philosophy, it may be best here to recall his admonition 'Whereof a man cannot speak, thereof he should be silent'.
Buried St Giles Cemetery, **Cambridge.**

YORKE, Philip, 1st earl of Hardwicke (1690-1764), Lord Chancellor. A handsome man with a good voice, best known for proscribing the tartan after the '45. A Whig, he supported Robert Walpole (see Norfolk) and held office under the Duke of Newcastle. He bought the great showplace Wimpole Hall from Edward Harley, 1st earl of Oxford, the hall being sold to pay off Harley's huge debts.

Yorke family monuments in **Wimpole** chapel. 1st earl's huge: his son, Charles (1722-1770) also there. Charles' brilliant early career was set back by his running battle with John Wilkes. He supported William Pitt, but was disappointed with him after Pitt was made Lord Chatham. After hesitating, accepted the Lord Chancellor ship (like his father) through ambition, though honour might have prompted him to decline in the circumstances - the emotional upset involved in deciding so affected his health that he soon died. 3rd earl in marble, and others.

Also brasses and alabaster tomb of Sir Thomas Chichele (1666), who began Hall.

The 4th earl, Charles Philip, became an admiral and impressed Queen Victoria by attentiveness during a royal shipboard visit. He entertained the Queen and Prince Albert at Wimpole in 1843 when, having mislaid her jewels, she came to the dinner table with a wreath of roses in her hair, inspiring admiring comments.

Incidentally, according to Edward Mace of The Observer, when enormous Wimpole Hall was lived in by Mrs Elsie Bambridge, Rudyard Kipling's daughter, he said to her on his first visit, "You've taken a lot on, haven't you, Elsie?"

Essex

ADAMS (née Flower), Sarah (1805-48), poet. Wrote 'Nearer, my God, to Thee' and other hymns, for which her sister Eliza composed the music. Attractive and high-spirited, as well as high-minded, Sarah was the daughter of a radical Nonconformist journalist who was visited, while in Newgate prison for his political activities, by Eliza Gould, who shared his outlook. On his release they married and he set up as a printer in Harlow. Sarah married William Brydges Adams in 1834; he encouraged her to go on the stage, but ill-health forced her to retire and she turned to verse. Besides devotional poems, she wrote verses for the Anti-Corn Law League. She lived at Woodbury Hill, Loughton.
Buried in Baptist graveyard, Foster Street, near **Harlow.**

ALLEN, Benjamin (1663-1738), physician and naturalist. Met John Ray after claiming discovery of winged glow-worms about 1692. On Ray's admission Allen cured him of jaundice by an infusion of stallion's dung in beer. Allen practised as a physician in Braintree. For remedies recorded in Allen's Commonplace Book, see Addison's *Worthies,* as for other details including an assessment of Allen's natural history of medicinal waters in England.
Like Ray, Allen was buried at **Black Notley.**

AUDLEY, Thomas, Lord Audley (1488-1544), Lord Chancellor. 'Mind your liver' is the popular translation of the Audley motto 'Garde ta Foy' (Keep your faith) over the gateway to the hall of Magdalene College, Cambridge, which Audley refounded. He rose with Wolsey and kept rising in Henry VIII's favour. He helped get rid of Catherine of Aragon, then Anne

Boleyn and Catherine Howard, also Bishop Fisher and Sir Thomas More, whom he replaced as Lord Chancellor. He profited enormously from the dissolution of the monasteries.

'The stone is not harder nor the marble blacker than the heart of him who lies beneath', commented the 17th century church historian, 'the worthy Dr Fuller', on the Audley monument of black Tournai marble in **Saffron Walden** church

The great house of Audley End was built by Thomas' grandson, Thomas, 1st earl of Suffolk. "Too large for a king," James I said of it, "but it might do for a lord treasurer."

BARNARDO, Dr Thomas John (1845-1905), philanthrophist. Born in Dublin and became a clerk. His religious conversion in 1862 led to evangelising work in the Dublin slums. He became a medical student in London in 1866 and about that time, horrified by conditions in London slums, Barnardo decided to devote his life to the care of friendless and destitute children. He first helped boys in the East End of London, then girls (beginning at Mossford Lodge, Barkingside, a wedding present). In the 1870s he was criticised for profiting from his charitable enterprises, a charge he vigorously and successfully refuted, though some have considered him dictatorial. 'No destitute child ever refused admission' became the boast of the network of children's homes he founded. In his lifetime he saved 60,000 children, helped 250,000 more - many sent to Canada for farm training and settlement. A friend and associate of 'General' William Booth.

Barnardo buried in his village Children's Church, **Barkingside.**

*BAYNARD, Ralph, 11th century lord of Little Dunmow. Supposed that his wife or sister founded the Priory there in 1104 and instituted the award of a flitch of bacon to couples who had not quarrelled or repented of their marriage for a year. First known award in 1404. Chair (from 14th century stall) in the church is claimed to be the one used to carry the

winners on a triumphal progress. The long and narrow
church of **Little Dunmow** was a chapel of the Priory.
There are alabaster effigies of Walter, Lord Fitzwalter
(1432) and his wife (1464). Some say the Fitzwalters
introduced the award from Normandy or Brittany.
*In 1855 the novelist Harrison Ainsworth revived the
flitch ceremony and it was transferred to Great
Dunmow.*

BLACKMORE, Sir Richard (died 1729), writer, physician
in ordinary to William III and Queen Anne. Knighted
1697. Wrote on medical matters and much else. His
verse is not highly thought of these days, though in the
18th century his literary reputation was generally high,
at least as far as his religious output was concerned.
Blackmore's *Creation*, 1712, drew tributes from Addison
and Dr Johnson. Even in his lifetime, however, there
were dissenting voices. *Eliza, an Epic Poem in X
Books*, 1705, for instance, failed to arouse much
enthusiasm; indeed, John Dryden, who accused Blackmore of plagiarism, wrote that his couplets were composed 'to the rumble of his coach's wheels'.
Blackmore was buried at St Peter's, **Boxted,** its Norman
tower being built of the conglomerate pudding-stone.

BLEWITT, Mrs Martha (died 1681) of the Swan Inn at
Balthorn End. Was the wife of nine husbands
successively, but No.9 survived her. The text at her
funeral service was 'Last of all, the Woman died also'.
The same tombstone mentions Robert Hogan who
married the last of his seven wives on New Year's Day,
1739 - 16 spouses between the pair! Mrs Blewitt and
Hogan buried at **Birdbrook,** an attractive village with a
delightful church containing good modern woodwork and
glass.

*BOLEYN, Ann (1507-36), Henry VIII's second queen,
mother of Elizabeth I. Returning from three years at
the French court, her gaiety and charm, if not perhaps
her swarthy complexion, long neck and wide mouth,
turned Henry's thoughts from Catherine of Aragon. But
he wanted to be rid of Ann in her turn after she failed
to bear a son and he had her executed. On the scaffold

she spanned her long neck with her fingers, saying to the headsman that it was small enough.

Legend has it that her severed head was smuggled to **East Horndon** and buried under the altar tomb in the south transept wall of All Saints' Church.

The village has developed away from the all-brick church, leaving it somewhat isolated and closed for regular services, but it is nevertheless memorable for its unique structure of an upper room above each transept, forming small galleries. It has Tyrrell family associations, a 16th century chantry and an incised stone slab of 1422.

BOUDICCA [BOADICEA in Latin form], queen of the Iceni (died c.62). The Romans tried to exploit the Iceni after Boudicca's husband Prasatugas died, she protested and thereupon was flogged, her daughters raped. Boudicca roused neighbouring tribes, took Camulodumum [Colchester], burned London and destroyed Verulamium [near St Albans]. The Roman governor Suetonius hastened from reducing the Druid stronghold of Mona [Anglesey] and, at last, Boudicca's forces were defeated.
There are many legends about her end. One says she took poison after a last stand at Ambresbury Banks in Epping Forest; another that the barrows of the **Bartlow Hills** mark her grave and those of the Iceni royal house. For the record, Boudicca is sometimes said to be buried under Platform 10, King's Cross Station, London, which is in an area formerly called Battle Bridge - the battle being, in this version, Boudicca's last stand.

BOURCHIER, Henry, earl of Essex (died 1483), Treasurer 1455, 1461 and 1471. His connections suggest that he would have strongly supported the Yorkists in the Wars of the Roses, since he married Edward IV's aunt and, indeed, received various estates from the King, but he did his best to be impartial. The Paston (see Norfolk) Letters mention Bourchier's opposing John de Vere, Earl of Oxford's landing at St Osyth in 1473 and forcing him to re-embark.
Bourchier originally buried at Beeleigh Abbey, **Maldon,** but reinterred in 1536 at **Little Easton.**

BRIGHT, Edward (1721-50), 'the biggest man in England'. Stood 5ft 9in tall, weighing over 42 stone, yet surprisingly active. Seven grown men were buttoned inside his waistcoat without bursting a stitch or straining a button. Many interesting details in Stan Jarvis' *View*. When Bright was buried a special apparatus had to be rigged up in the church.
Buried All Saints, **Maldon,** church with brick Gothic nave and unique 13th century triangular tower.
In the 17th century the Nonconformist minister, Joseph Billio, was so continually active that his name is proverbial - 'doing something like billio.'
Maldon is attractive, slanting up from the waterside promenade on the Blackwater. A port and yachting harbour, famous for oysters. The Battle of Maldon is mentioned under Byrtnoth (Cambridgeshire).

BROWNE, Sir Antony (1510-67), judge, founder of Brentwood School. In 1555 Browne was a commissioner, like Lord Rich, to enforce the Statute of Heretics against Puritans. Some say Browne had no fixed religious opinions, others claim he was active in persecuting Protestants: he certainly ordered the arrest of young William Hunter in 1555. The next year, at all events, Browne was knighted by Elizabeth. In 1557 he bought a piece of land to extend Brentwood School - 'the Grammar School of Antony Browne, Sergeant at Law, in Brentwood' - first built 1568. He was appointed Chief Justice in 1558, later removed, but continuing as a judge.
Buried **South Weald,** in the medieval church, one of an attractive group of buildings.

BUSS, Frances Mary (1827-94), pioneer of girls' education. She died of overwork: no wonder! She faced incredible hostility - study was alleged to be beyond girls' intellectual capacities, it would check their menstruation and was contrary to the divine plan. Miss Buss taught from the age of 14, at first in her mother's little private school, which she reorganised as North London Collegiate School, a model for future High Schools for girls. She taught Anne Clough (see Cambridgeshire) and supported the founding of

Newnham. By example, exhortation and argument she helped many educational reforms, from teachers' pensions to qualifications for women teachers. An associate of Dorothea Beale, the famous principal of Cheltenham Ladies' College. Frances Buss was amused by the rhyme 'Miss Buss and Beale/ Cupid's darts do not feel;/ How different from us,/ Miss Beale and Miss Buss'; said to have been written on a blackboard at her school.
Buried **Theydon Bois.**
In the adjoining parish of Theydon Mount the 16th century Hill Hall is said to be haunted by a grey-haired *In the adjoining parish of Theydon Mount the 16th century Hill Hall is said to be haunted by a grey-haired woman, a phantom black dog and a phantom mustard-coloured coach. It is also supposedly the scene, early in its history, of a seven-cornered duel between seven brothers who courted a beautiful girl at the Hall unable to make up her mind which to marry. They fought in her presence and every brother was killed.*

BYNG, Julian Hedworth George, Viscount Byng of Vimy (1862-1935), soldier and administrator. A very long and distinguished active service, first in Sudan and then the Boer War. In the Great War he took part in the first battle of Ypres, next sent in 1915 to command the IX Corps in Gallipoli. He commanded the Canadian Army Corps, 1916-17, with the peak of his career coming when Vimy Ridge was captured in 1917. Went on to command the Third Army, 1917-18. His Canadian associations continued with his appointment as Governor -General of Canada, 1921-26. As Chief Commissioner of the Metropolitan Police Byng introduced many reforms, from improved patrolling to the extended use of police cars and the institution of police telephone boxes.
Buried **Beaumont-cum-Moze** (Moze meaning marsh).

BYRD, William (1543-1623), composer. 'Bred up to music,' Byrd said, by Thomas Tallis, with whom he was organist at the Chapel Royal, despite being a Catholic. After 1585 he had the monopoly of selling music and music paper, previously shared with Tallis. He came to be a friend of the Petre family, who may have aided him. Byrd turned out to be one of the greatest of the Tudor composers. He lived for 30 years at Stondon Massey, near Ongar, buying the lease of Stondon Place in 1593 from a fellow Roman Catholic, William Shelley, after the Crown had confiscated what was then a farmhouse; Shelley's aggrieved widow failed to get the house back. Byrd wanted to be buried next to his wife at **Stondon Massey;** perhaps he was. A mural tablet was erected to him on his tercentary, in the church with a Norman body, housing a 17th century pulpit and reader's desk. *The village has a combined signpost and whipping post.*

CANFIELD, Benet, see Fitch, William.

CANHAM, Catherine (Kitty) (1720-72), bigamist. She married the Vicar of Thorpe-le-Soken and then mysteriously disappeared. Her husband was further mystified to hear she had become a viscountess. Somewhere John, Lord Dalmeny, met her, fell in love and married her without knowing she already had a husband. They travelled through Europe together until Kitty fell mortally ill in Verona, leaving a death-bed confession containing a wish to be buried at Thorpe. Her body was embalmed for the devoted Lord Dalmeny and transported across Europe. In the Channel the ship was boarded by Customs Officers who, intent upon finding contraband, insisted on opening the chest containing the body: explanations demanded and given. Happyish ending - Kitty was indeed buried at **Thorpe-le-Soken,** in the presence of both widowers. *Church rebuilt, has 15th century brick tower and chapel screen.*

*CAVELL, Edith (1865-1915), nurse shot by German authorities. **Steeple Bumpstead** church has a tablet to 'Nurse Cavell, murdered at Brussels, October 12, 1915. Some time a worshipper in this church' (See also Norfolk). *The River Colne rises not far from Steeple Bumpstead's 11th century tower and chancel.*

CHAMBERLEN, Dr Peter (1601-83), surgeon. Of Huguenot stock, Chamberlen was a successful obstetrician, thanks at least in part to the use of a special forceps, a family secret (their use much criticised). Physician in ordinary to Charles I and Charles II. Bought Dutch-gabled Woodham Mortimer Hall; some obstetrical instruments were found there in 1818.

His son Hugo also court physician, but unlucky; he arrived too late to deliver the heir to James II and, when in 1692, he delivered Princess Anne of a son, the child immediately died. Dr Hugo Chamberlen proposed in 1694 that taxation should be levied for a national medical service.

He erected a tomb chest honouring his father in **Woodham Mortimer** churchyard.

CHILD, Sir Josiah (1630-99), merchant and economist. Very interesting details in Addison's *Worthies*. Child's father was a prosperous London merchant. Josiah succeeded to the family business, becoming victualler to the navy about 1655 and amassing a fortune of £200,000 apparently through systematic bribery. Elected to Parliament in 1659, he invested most of his money in the East India Company, being made a director in 1677 and later governor. He advocated reduction in interest, setting out his theories in *A New Discourse of Trade*, 1690. Child impressed the diarist John Evelyn by the scale of developments to his estate, Wanstead Park.

A quite outstanding monument to Sir Josiah, with full bottomed wig, but otherwise garbed as a Roman, with other figures recumbent and standing, in **Wanstead** Old Church (St Mary's), rebuilt 1790, Tuscan porch, bell turret, box pews, and an outstanding pulpit whose sounding board rests on two palm trees.

Sir Josiah's son, Sir Richard Child, continued to develop Wanstead Park. Further work by descendant 2nd Earl Tylney.

CHRISTY, Miller (1861-1928), naturalist and historian. He 'lies quite forgotten and unremarked', Jarvis, *View:* a pity, for as Jarvis shows, Christy was an interesting character. For instance, he researched Essex hearings of

artillery fire on the Western Front during the Great
War. Educated at the Quaker School, Epping. His first
book was a natural history of Canada after service with
Tuke Commission for settling Irish in Manitoba. Then
many books and articles about Essex. Christy early
showed curiosity about industrial archaeology. He was
an active field naturalist and a founder of the Essex
Field Club. He collaborated with his friend Ernest
Thompson Seton and contributed to the *Dictionary of
National Biography*. His *Birds of Essex*, 1890, remained standard for many years. In 1894 Christy edited
the voyages of Foxe and James for the Hakluyt Society.
Buried **Chignall St James,** 'a plain and humble church in
a small place' (Jarvis).

CLAYPOOLE (or CLAYPOLE). Mr George D Kissell
drew my attention to an entry in the register of St
Mary's Church, **Walthamstow:**
'Dec.1674. Yr was buried a child of Mr Claypoole's,
son-in-law to Oliver Cromwell (late Protector of
England, Scotland and Ireland).'
Mr Kissell added: 'This inscription is in delicate
writing, but the words in parenthesis have been rudely
scored out by a later hand, probably after the Restoration. Claypoole lived for a time at The Chestnuts, Hoe
Street, Walthamstow, a building still in use for
teaching.'
Perhaps the child was Henry Claypoole, who died before
his elder brother Cromwell (1678). The third son,
Oliver, died 1658. Daughter Martha died 1664.

COMYNS, Sir John (1667-1740), judge. Highly successful
in his day, now largely forgotten except for those
stirred to wonder about him by his monument, which
records that he tried to raise a family with each of
three wives in turn, but in vain. He served Maldon as
MP on several occasions, 1701-26. Baron of the
Exchequer in 1728, later transferred to Court of
Common Pleas, then back to Exchequer as Lord Chief
Baron in 1739.
Bust and fine monument in the parish church, **Writtle.**
*The village, on the River Wid, has a pleasant green and
also an agricultural college. Before the church are two*

attractive houses, one 16th century, timbered, but much restored, the other, 17th century, has an unusual front door, shell-hooded.

COOKE, Sir Anthony (1504-76), tutor to Edward VI, who made him Knight of the Bath. Lady Jane Grey joined his four daughters for lessons given by the scholarly Sir Anthony, who devoted much time to their education. The association with Lady Jane brought Cooke to the Tower, but he was released in 1554 and fled to Strasbourg with Sir John Cheke, until Elizabeth came to the throne and he could return safely to England. His daughter Mildred married William Cecil (see Cambridgeshire) as his second wife; his second daughter Anne married Sir Nicholas Bacon (second wife) and was mother of Francis Bacon. Sir Anthony's grandfather began the building of the first (fortified) Gidea Hall, Romford; Sir Anthony completed it.
Alabaster monument to him in **Romford** parish church. Others of the family buried there.

*CORNWELL, Jack, VC (1900-16). At the naval battle of Jutland Cornwell was mortally injured, but stood by his gun, being posthumously awarded the Victoria Cross. This former van boy's old school in East Ham was renamed Cornwell Secondary Modern School after him and children collected for his monument in Manor Park Cemetary, **East Ham.** There are homes named after Cornwell in Hornchurch.

COURTAULD, Samuel (1793-1881), industrialist. Silk was what the Courtauld family first specialised in at several Essex mills. The business expanded enormously under Samuel until, in 1846, a tent was set up outside his home for a dinner for him and his associates by 1,600 workers. The family home was Bocking Place. Braintree owes its town hall, hospital, fountains and much else to the Courtaulds. Family business later turned to producing rayon and set up an international concern. They established the rayon industry in the U S A in 1909, but sold much of their investment during World War II to gain dollar credit for Britain.

Samuel Courtauld is buried **Gosfield,** where the church, in a fine setting, has an unusual squire's pew like a theatre box. The Courtauld family restored and added to Gosfield Hall, originally a Tudor courtyard house; much altered in 18th century, it has a long gallery with Tudor panels and a secret chamber.

Another Samuel Courtauld (1876-1947) was a remarkable patron of the arts (not the only one in the family), giving the Tate Gallery £50,000 for French paintings in 1923 and, with Viscount Lee of Farnham, founding the Courtauld Institute of Art for London University in 1932 after his wife's death.

*CRIPPS, Rev. Arthur Stanley (1869-1952), missionary. Worked in Southern Rhodesia, a name which he, as a champion of native rights, disliked and tried to avoid. The diocese of Mashonaland gave a memorial to **Ford End,** Great Waltham, where Cripps was twice vicar, first from 1895 to 1900 and again 1927-30. He served as a missionary in the interim and again after 1930. Memorial represents the Crucifixion with native Africans in the three main roles.

*CRITTALL, Francis Henry (1860-1935), metal window frame manufacturer. Dismayed when his mother strained herself trying to lift a heavy wooden window frame, so the story goes, Crittall devised metal frames, which were highly successful. Though unconfirmed, the story exemplifies Crittall's care for others. Large-scale production of metal windows by his firm was made possible by a craftsman's success in devising a better window. Throughout, Crittall kept the support of his employees. He was much concerned for their welfare, paying well above average wages, introducing the closed shop policy (the first engineering firm to do so) in support of trade union activity, ending Saturday working, providing training and social facilities. He created the garden village of Silver End for his workers, aiming at a self-supporting community. Included was a factory for disabled workers. Progressive architects were employed and some fo the flat-roofed houses were singled out for mention by Pevsner in his volume on Essex buildings. During the Great War Crittall went into munitions and opposed any idea of profiteering. He played little part in local affairs, although a JP from 1904; his business was his life.

Crittall died on board ship, returning from a Caribbean cruise, and was cremated at Golders Green. A memorial garden, with decorative gates and lamps made by the workpeople, was opened at **Silver End** in 1950.

*CUNOBELINUS, 1st century AD king of the Catevellauni. Shakespeare used him as Cymbeline. Under his rule the Catevellauni, a Belgic people, dominated southeastern England. He made Colchester his capital as Camulodunum (from the name of his war-god).

Often claimed that Cunobelinus was commemorated in the imposing barrow in **Lexden Park,** Colchester, from which treasures now in Colchester Museum were recovered.

Colchester, associated with Old King Cole, is said to be Britain's oldest recorded town. Claudius recognised its importance and built a temple. Boudicca burnt it in 60. There are extensive Roman walls. The Norman Castle, built 1085, above Roman temple. John Ball, dreamer of social equality, was rector of St James's; barbarously executed, Richard II looking on.

DAY, Daniel (died 1767), pump-maker. An eccentric from Wapping, Day used to invite his friends to an annual feast of beans and bacon in Hainault Forest, under the huge and venerable Fairlop Oak. The party would travel in a wooden boat on wheels, drawn by six horses. The event developed into an annual fair centred round the Oak: at last a branch fell from the tree and Day took this as an omen of his death and had the wood made into a coffin, which he tested for size before he died.

Buried **Barking** churchyard.

Plaque near Fairlop Oak Inn, Barkingside, said to mark the site of the fair, abolished 1843.

de VERE family, Earls of Oxford. Supported the Empress Maud, who gave them the Oxford title.

Aubrey de Vere (c.1090-1114), King's Chamberlain.

Founded priory at Hatfield Broad Oak, then built the finest rectangular keep in England, four storeys high, at Castle Hedingham. Buried **Earl's Colne** (good tower on 14th century church, restored).
So too were the following:
5th earl - at least his body, for his heart was buried at Ipswich;
7th earl, who led the English archers at Poitiers (1356);
9th earl, who accompanied Richard II to Mile End to meet Wat Tyler's men (1381);
13th earl, Henry VIII piled honours on him, but fined him for keeping too large a private army.
In 1935 several Oxford tombs were removed across the Suffolk border (see Suffolk entry) to St Stephen's Chapel.
3rd earl of Oxford, for one, preferred burial at **Hatfield Priory** - he was among the barons at the signing of the Magna Carta.
Later earls interred at **Castle Hedingham:**
15th earl, who took part in Wolsey's downfall and in the deposition of Catherine of Aragon. He carried Anne Boleyn's crown and was at her trial: present with Henry VIII at Blackheath for the reception of Anne of Cleves;
16th earl, the first Protestant earl.
Castle Hedingham church, with Norman nave, had a brick tower added 1616. The 12th century churchyard cross has been restored.
The de Vere connection with Essex ended in 1625.

DERHAM, Rev. William (1657-1735), horologist. A strong, healthy and amiable man, Derham had interests ranging from natural history to mechanics. He collected birds and insects and edited the works of John Ray. Made a Fellow of the Royal Society in 1702, he contributed to *Transactions*. Chaplain to the Prince of Wales, afterwards George II, later Canon of Windsor. Wrote *The Artificial Clockmaker* in 1696, used by Sir Walter Scott for *The Fortunes of Nigel*. Derham used the tower of Upminster church for scientific experiments, cutting a door in the wooden belfry to study stars and test echo-sounding. He timed gun-flashes

St Laurence, Upminster

from Blackheath, using a pendulum clock. He conducted many other experiments, some with apparatus lent by friends.
Buried in the chancel of **Upminster** church, which has a fine 13th century tower.

DIMSDALE, Thomas (1712-1800), pioneer of inoculation. Already a Fellow of the Royal Society when he published his first paper, highly successful, on inoculation in 1767. He became a wealthy physician and surgeon at Hertford. A Quaker friend recommended him to go to St Petersburg in 1768 to inoculate Catherine the Great and her son against smallpox: gratifying results - lavishly rewarded with £10,000 as a gift, annuity of £500 and other presents and made Baron.
Buried Friends' Burial Ground, **Bishop's Stortford,** where his grandfather, who went with William Penn to America in 1684, had practice.

DOUBLEDAY, Henry (1808-75), naturalist. Unsuccessful as a grocer and hardware dealer in Epping, but with a high reputation as an ornitholist and, especially, entomologist. Collected (and stuffed) birds, studied migrants. His brother Edward, also interested in natural history, observed the attraction of empty sugar barrels for moths, inspiring Henry to collect moths by brushing 'sugar water' on the bark of trees. An original member of the Entomological Society. Henry discovered true oxlip at Great Bradfield, grew it from seed and sent specimens to the *Gardeners' Chronicle* to prove the plant's existence in Britain. By 1871 forced to sell some of his collections to pay his debts. He had a nervous breakdown and was admitted to The Retreat, a Quaker institution in York, some friends providing as much financial support as they could.
Buried behind Friends' Meeting House, **Epping.**

EDWARDS, George (1693-1773), naturalist. A businessman until 1716, when he set off on his travels, drawing natural objects which seemed significant to him by their occurence in undisturbed surroundings. He attracted the attention of Sir Hans Sloane, who, in

1733, recommended Edwards as librarian to the Royal College of Physicians. By studying books there Edwards made himself a recognised ornithologist. He wrote several books, some of them in more than one volume. A Fellow of the Royal Society and the Society of Antiquaries, also member of various learned societies in Europe.

Buried **West Ham.** Addison notes in his account of Edwards in *Worthies* that the gravestone is missing.

FITCH, William. He has a brass in **Little Canfield** church, but it is his son of the same name who has come to renewed attention, thanks to Aldous Huxley, as Addison notes in *Worthies.* The son is known as Benet Canfield (1563-1611) and was a mystic, author of *The Rule of Perfection,* which sets out his method of prayer and which Huxley described in *Grey Eminence.*

The younger William Fitch joined the Franciscans at Douai in 1586 as Brother Benedict of Canfield. He returned to England after three years, but was arrested and imprisoned, first in the Tower, then in Wisbech Castle. In 1592 Henry IV of France succeeded in obtaining his release, Canfield thereupon returning to France, where he was appointed Master of Novices and Guardian of the Convent at Rouen, where he died.

FRY (née Gurney) Mrs Elizabeth (1780-1845), prison reformer. The daughter of Norfolk Quaker banker John Gurney, she married London merchant Joseph Fry. Her sister Hannah married Sir Thomas Fowell Buxton (see Norfolk). Elizabeth started a school for girls ('Betsy's imps') in East Ham after her husband inherited the Plashet estate there. She had already, when only 15, tried to improve conditions for women prisoners in Norwich. After 1813 prison work at Newgate and other jails and efforts to improve the lot of criminals transported to New South Wales, the London homeless and beggars in Brighton. In 1841 visited Copenhagen and toured French prisons that year. Frederick William of Prussia admired her work and visited her at West Ham in 1842 to tell her so.

Buried Friends' Burial Ground, **Barking,** like her brother Samuel Gurney.

FRYATT, Captain Charles Algernon (1872-1916), sailor. Sailed between Harwich and the continent in Great Eastern Railway Company ships. During the Great War Fryatt was chased by a U-boat, but turned on it and tried to ram it, forcing it to submerge. The Germans mounted a big operation to capture him, court-martialled him as a franc-tireur, condemned and shot him, despite U.S. minister's protests. Verdict widely held to be grossly illegal.
Body returned to churchyard at **Dovercourt** after the War. The Great Eastern Railway erected a monument; another monument to him on Mount Fryatt, Alberta, Canada.
All Saints Church, Dovercourt, has a lych gate presented by Queen Victoria as a memorial to soldiers of the 1809 Walcheren expedition and the church also has a window given by Kaiser Wilhelm II of Germany commemorating Germans from the same expedition, buried, like the British, in the churchyard.

GILBERT (sometimes GILBERD), Dr William (1544-1603), physician and natural philosopher. Born in Colchester, son of a Recorder. He made a great success as a medical practitioner in London, physician to Elizabeth I and James I, president of the College of Physicians, 1600. He has a far greater reputation as the author of *De Magnete,* an investigation of the properties of the magnet, the first important study of physics in England, laying the foundations of the science of electricity. Gilbert introduced the terms 'electricity', 'electric force' and 'electric attraction'. He argued in favour of experimental evidence and established the magnetic nature of the earth, realised that the moon is responsible for the tides, suggested that electricity and terrestrial magnetism were allied emanations of a single force and showed that, when rubbed, substances other than amber attract light objects. The gilbert, unit of magneto-motive power, is named after him. Gilbert's merit at once recognised at home and on the continent, drawing praise from Galileo, for instance.
Buried Holy Trinity Church, **Colchester.**

GODFREY, Sir Edmund (1621-78), victim of unsolved murder. A prosperous merchant dealing in coal and timber, Godfrey was a London JP, very conscientious, undeterred even by the Plague and the Great Fire. Charles II was appreciative and knighted him. Godfrey was caught up in the scheming of those behind Titus Oates, who made a deposition before Godfrey in 1678 alleging a Popish plot. Godfrey was found, murdered, on Primrose Hill within weeks; many theories, none fully satisfactory, as to why he was killed.

Monumental column in **Woodford** churchyard. Other Godfrey memorials, including Michael Godfrey (1658-95), a founder of the Bank of England.

GOLDING, Arthur (1536?-1605?), translator of classics, including Caesar, Seneca and Ovid. Perhaps best known for his version in 14 syllable lines of Ovid's *Metamorphoses*, 1565 and 1567, which contains a preface setting out the moral meaning of the stories. Many Elizabethans used Golding's translation as a source of mythological knowledge: Shakespeare took subject matter from it and borrowed phrases, e.g. for Prospero's last speech in *The Tempest*.

Like other Goldings, buried **Belchamp St Paul,** a church which has misericorde seats, rare in Essex.

GRANTHAM, Nathaniel (died 1723), sailor. Little is known of the life of this naval commander, but, by chance, a little more about his burial at **West Thurrock.** In 1906 the rector, Rev. W J Hayes, was breaking down a wall to enlarge a vault when he came across a lead coffin. On turning back some of the lead he found a man's body inside, surprisingly well preserved. The coffin contained a good deal of liquid, that the rector boldly decided to taste, although it had presumably been used for pickling the corpse. Knowing the pickled man's profession, we may not be as surprised as the rector when he discovered the liquid was rum!

GREVILLE (née Maynard), Frances, Countess of Warwick (1861-1938), society beauty and socialist. Mistress, 1889-98, of Edward, prince of Wales (Edward VII), who called her 'my own adored little Daisy Wife'.

The Prince's letters to her burned after she asked George V for £100,000 for them; a scandal was prevented by Arthur du Cros, who himself paid off her £48,000 debts. Elinor Glyn made her the heroine of a novel. She married in 1881 Francis Richard Charles Guy Greville, Lord Brooke, later 5th earl of Warwick. The socialist Robert Blatchford criticised her extravagance, stirred her conscience and she became a passionate socialist herself just before ceasing to be the Prince's mistress. Founded secondary school at Dunmow, also a women's agricultural college. Stood unsuccessfully as Labour candidate against Anthony Eden in 1923 at Warwick. She founded a nature sanctuary at Easton Lodge (now demolished), inherited from grandfather. Many distinguished literary and socialist figures came to visit her.

Opulent monument (she is 'in very Edwardian costume and attitude', Pevsner) in Bourchier or Maynard Chapel, **Little Easton** church.

GULL, Sir William Withey (1816-90), physician. Lurid rumour hangs over his later life, but he began sunnily enough. In royal favour for his successful treatment of the Prince of Wales' typhoid in 1871, he was created physician in ordinary to the Queen in 1882. A gifted teacher, good public speaker and attentive doctor. The great fortune he earned seemed justified.

Grave at **Thorpe-le-Soken;** but was he buried there? Was the coffin filled with stones? Was, in fact, Sir William Gull really Jack the Ripper, safe at last in a private asylum after hideously murdering East End prostitutes? Queries not tested by opening the grave.

GURNEY, Samuel (1786-1856), banker and philanthropist. Tried to relieve Irish famine victims, 1849. A town in Liberia was named after him in 1851 for his generosity. He worked on penal reform with his brother Joseph John, Sir Thomas Fowell Buxton (see Norfolk) and his sister Elizabeth Fry. It was Joseph Fry who gave Samuel a start in his counting-house in 1800. Gurney joined another counting-house, Richardson and Overend, in 1807 and shared its phenomenal success. In

1825 the house became Overend and Gurney, its reputation higher than that of the Bank of England and its funds sufficient for it to lend money to other banks if needed; hence Gurney was known as 'the bankers' banker'.
Buried, like Elizabeth Fry, in the Friends' Burial Ground, **Barking.**

HADDOCK, Sir Richard (1629-1715), admiral. Charles II took off his silken cap and put it on Haddock's head: that was when Haddock was presented to the King for bravery while commanding the *Royal James*, flagship of the Earl of Sandwich at the Battle of Sole Bay against the Dutch in 1672. Charles' gesture was remarkable for permitting a subject to appear with his head covered in the royal presence, even more remarkable in an age when men, especially of rank, were rarely seen in public without headgear. Haddock was subsequently knighted and given a succession of appointments, from First Commissioner of the Victualling Office to joint commander-in-chief (one of three) of an expedition against Ireland.
Buried St Clement's Church, **Leigh-on-Sea,** now a residential resort, but in Haddock's time (and after) a hamlet dependent on fishing and smuggling.

HALL, Chester Moor (1703-71), inventor of the achromatic lens, c.1733, solving a problem that Newton had declared unsolvable. Hall was led to his discovery by studying the human eye. A wealthy land-owner, bencher of the Honourable Society of the Inner Temple and an amateur astronomer, Hall did not make his achievement public. In 1758 the optician John Dollond was given the Copley Medal for invention of the achromatic lens, though not yet a member of the Royal Society. In 1766 Dollond's son, Peter, brought an action for infringement of patent; his opponent, Champion, defended on the grounds that Hall had made a similar instrument. Lord Mansfield nevertheless ruled Dollond the inventor, since Hall had 'confined the discovery to his closet'.
Hall's sister erected a marble monument to him in the chancel of **Sutton** church, which has a typical Essex weatherboarded belfry.

HAROLD II, Godwinsson (c.1022-66), King of England. As Earl of Wessex, effectively ruler of England under Edward the Confessor. Fought the Welsh and ravaged Wales 1062. Accepted the crown in 1066 despite an oath to help Duke William of Normandy to English throne. Repulsed Norwegian invasion, September, 1066, killing the great Viking Harald Hardraada, then marching to Hastings to face William, but was killed (14 October, 1066), as the Bayeux Tapestry shows.

Persistent legend says that Harold was buried behind the high altar of the huge church he completed in 1060 at **Waltham** (later monastery and abbey) and a modern stone in the Abbey churchyard marks the site.

The surviving Norman nave has been compared with the nave of Durham Cathedral. Queen Eleanor's body rested at Waltham on its way to Westminster. Thomas Fuller (1608-61), the church historian and antiquarian, was curate of Waltham Abbey, c.1648, and wrote a history. Later, the Waltham bells are said to have inspired passages of In Memoriam *while Tennyson was living at Beech Hill House, 1837-40.*

HARSNETT, Samuel (1561-1631), archbishop of York. A High Churchman with a low opinion of himself - in Chigwell church his fine brass, the latest of those to a bishop, says 'he was formerly vicar here, then the unworthy bishop of Chichester, next the more unworthy bishop of Norwich and lastly the very unworthy archbishop of York'. Many Puritans agreed, including the Fellows of Pembroke College, Cambridge, where he was Master. Harsnett founded Chigwell Grammar School in 1629 as thanks for appointment as archbishop. From Harsnett's pamphlet vigorously exposing 'popish designs' Shakespeare took the names of spirits mentioned by Edgar in *King Lear*, and scholars find phrasing inspired by Harsnett in Milton's 'L'Allegro'.

Buried at **Chigwell.** Harsnett's brass, set high, is not easy to see.

The Maypole public house in Barnaby Rudge *is said to have been drawn from the King's Head Inn, Chigwell.*

HARVEY, Sir Eliab (1758-1830), admiral. Short-tempered, apt to kick his wig about and use nautical language. Naval service from boyhood, interrupted in 1780 when he inherited a fortune with a family estate at Hempstead and took to gambling and a busy social life. Resumed active service when war with France broke out in 1793: commanded Sea Fencibles in Essex in 1797. In West Indies, then commissioned in the *Fighting Temeraire;* his exploits at Trafalgar earned him promotion to rear-admiral. Harvey publicly criticised the promotion of Lord Cochrane, according to one account, and was dismissed, though reinstated 1810. An alternative version is that he was dismissed for criticising Admiral Lord Gambier for lack of enterprise in blockading the French coast. Harvey lost all his sons young, the eldest, Edward, fighting at Burgos 1812. In 1826 Harvey was MP for Essex.

Buried **Hempstead.**

The highwayman, Dick Turpin, supposedly born 1705 at the Crown Inn.

HARVEY, Gabriel (1545?-1630), scholar and poet. Some would prefer to describe him as pedant and poetaster, but at least he won and kept the friendship of Edmund Spenser. Harvey appears as Hobbinot in the *Shepheardes Calendar,* which is inscribed to him as 'the most learned both Orator and Poete'. He had a very high regard of himself, was ambitious and extremely quarrelsome. Embroiled in the Martin Marprelate pamphlet war between Puritans and Episcopalians, he provoked the highly gifted Thomas Nashe, who quite overwhelmed Harvey by sarcasm and invective.

Harvey was born and lived for much of his life in **Saffron Walden,** where he died and is said to be buried. *Tucked away in the south aisle of the great church of St Mary, in the spandrels of an arch, facing the great door, someone about 1495 carved a saffron crocus, symbol of the town, formerly extensively grown there for dyeing, for medicine and as a condiment. Church very large, very fine, akin architecturally to King's College, Cambridge. Ruined Norman castle; nearby perhaps the best earth maze in England. Houses and inns of much interest, in brick or brick and flint, some* *with pargetting (East Anglian decorative plasterwork).*

HARVEY, William (1578-1657), discoverer of the circulation of the blood. A little man, plagued 'much and
often' by gout which drove him to an heroic remedy
involving a pail of icy water for his legs on the roof of
his London house, whatever the weather. After studying
at Padua, Harvey commanded great respect as physician
to James I and Charles I and as Lumleian Lecturer at
the College of Physicians. Published his treatise on the
circulation of the blood in 1628 and demonstrated his
theory to Emperor Charles V at Nuremberg. Attended
Charles I at the battle of Edgehill, but sat under a
hedge reading a book until a near miss by a cannon
ball made him retire.
Harvey's body taken from London to **Hempstead,**
followed on foot by Fellows of the College of
Physicians. Buried in lead in family vault; in 1883 a
white marble sarcophagus was provided by the College.

HAWKWOOD, Sir John (died 1394), soldier of fortune.
Said to be the son of a Sible Hedingham tanner,
knighted by Edward III after fighting at Crecy and
Poitiers. He formed his White Company of freelances: in
Italy in 1360 his price was too high for Venice, but
they served the Pope, Pisa and Perugia and Hawkwood
became son-in-law of the Duke of Milan. At first he
fought against Florence, then sided with that city for
annual pension and defended it against Milan. Much
respected in Florence and was commemorated in the
Duomo by a Uccello painting. Wife given permission in
1385 to take his body back to **Sible Hedingham**, where
a tomb chest is pointed out as his; some see carvings
of hawks on the arch above it.
*Church has the royal arms of William and Mary carved
in wood.*

HOPKINS, Matthew (died 1647), 'witchfinder'. Used
torture while Witchfinder General in East Anglia,
earning 20 shillings for every town he visited. He had
29 persons condemned in one batch. At his peak he had
200 in gaol and 68 hanged. During the Cambridge trial
of Mrs Lendall, Hopkins said in court that a male

witch, Old Stranguidge, had flown over Great Shelford church on a black dog, 'tearing his breeches on the steeple weathervane' - the torn garment produced as evidence. Methods, but not principle, condemned by commission. Exposed by John Gaule, vicar of Great Slaughter, Huntingdonshire, a Royalist turned Parliamentarian (for which he paid at the Restoration). Some say Hopkins was himself tried and hanged; others that he retired to Manningtree, where he had unsuccessfully practised law, died unpunished and was buried at **Mistley.**

Church there rebuilt by Robert Adam, but only two towers remain. 18th century Swan Fountain commemorates the attempt to make Mistley a spa; there are many swans on the estuary of the Stour.

*HUNTER, William (1536?-55), Protestant martyr. Self-taught, Hunter appalled the vicar of Brentwood with his interpretation of the Communion. The vicar reported him to Sir Antony Browne, who ordered his arrest. Hunter fled; his father was sent after him and told the boy to escape, but he feared that if he did his father would be in trouble, so he gave himself up. Browne sent Hunter to London for examination as an heretic, he would not recant and was burned at the stake in Brentwood. Part of the tree at which he perished is in Brentwood School Museum.

Granite obelisk commemorating Hunter erected Shenfield Road, **Brentwood,** in 1861, rebuilt 1910 after damage by fire 1907.

White Hart and other old inns are a reminder that Brentwood was the first stage on the coaching road out of London.

JENKINS, 'Old Mother', 19th century white witch: the benevolent Goose Charmer of Epping Forest. See Murrell (Suffolk).

JENNENS, John (died 1769), claimant. Readers of *Bleak House* by Charles Dickens will recall the importance in the book of the Chancery suit 'Jarndyce v Jarndyce'.

Dickens based his terrible story on the dispute over the estates of William Jennens, of Acton Place, Suffolk. One of the claimants in that historical suit was John Jennens, who died in **Colchester.** Buried in St Peter's churchyard, under a tombstone inscribed 'Through deceit they refuse to know me'.

KEMPE, William (1555-1628), 'the silent man'. Silent because of remorse for having wrongly accused his wife of being unfaithful, so decided never to speak again. After seven years, terminally ill, he wanted to call for help, but found he was dumb, according to story. Lived at Spains Hall, Finchingfield, which had seven ponds in the garden, erroneously said to have been made by Kempe one a year to mark his silence.
Memorial in Kempe's Chapel, **Finchingfield** church, to him and his wife 'Philip' (died 1623).
The church has a lovely setting in a lovely village, its square Norman tower topped by an 18th century cupola. Also in the village are a green, a duck pond, a wind-mill, a former Guildhall (c.1500) and the thatched cottage called the Round House, which is hexagonal, dated late 18th century.

LAMB, Lynton [Harold] (1907-77), artist. Born in India, educated in Bath. Shared a studio with Victor Pasmore and was associated with the 'realist' Euston Road school of artists in its early days. On the staff of the Slade School 1950-71, Lamb was active in various fields, giving pleasure to many as a landscape genre painter, as lithographer and as engraver. He illustrated books and wrote about art: in 1955 he designed postage stamps and in 1959 designed the Purcell Memorial, Royal Festival Hall. President of the Society of Industrial Artists, 1951-3. Member of the Arts Panel, Arts Council, 1951-4.
Buried in the churchyard of St Andrew's, **Sandon,** and, appropriately, his painting of St Andrew hangs in the 16th century church, which has a brick tower.

LOCKE, John (1632-1704), philosopher. Three extra-ordinary achievements: established the case against divine right of kings and case for civil liberty*(Treatises* on *Government*, which influenced the American and French revolutionaries) and, in *Letters on Toleration*, argued for religious liberty. Locke was denied a medical degreee for political and religious reasons, but became physician to Ashley, later 1st earl of Shaftesbury, with whom he shared exile in France and Holland after Shaftesbury's downfall. Back in England, Locke went to High Laver for his chronic asthma, lived at Oates with Sir Francis Masham, paying one pound a week for his lodging and his man-servants.

Buried **High Laver;** tablet on inner south wall of church. As he lay dying, Locke listened to psalms read to him by Lady Damaris Masham (née Cudworth) (1658-1708), who had studied divinity under him. She, too, is buried in High Laver.

Here, later, two of the repatriated Tolpuddle Martyrs tried to farm, but were driven to emigrate to Canada with three others who had leased New House Farm, near Greensted.

LUCAS, Sir Charles (1613-48), Royalist. A cavalry commander, he served in the Civil War, attacking the Puritan Earl of Warwick (see Rich, Robert) at Leighs. Prominent in valiantly, but unsuccessfully, defending Colchester against besieging Parliamentary forces. Captured and shot with Sir George Lisle in castle yard. Buried in family vault in St Giles's Church, **Colchester;** so is Lisle.

MARTIN, Sarah Catherine (1768-1826), poet. The poem that brought her renown is 'Old Mother Hubbard' nursery rhyme, written about 1805. She was 17 when Prince William (later William IV) fell in love with her: after a year or so George III ended the association. The Prince consoled himself from 1790 with Mrs Jordan, who bore him 10 children up to 1811: Sarah Martin never married.

She is buried with her parents, Sir Harry and Lady Martin, in St Nicholas's churchyard (the church now in ruins), **Loughton,** near Loughton Hall.

The hiding place of the highwayman Dick Turpin (1705? -39), 'Turpin's Cave', still to be seen at High Beech, Loughton.

MASHAM (née Hill), Abigail, Lady Masham (died 1734), favourite of Queen Anne. A rather plain woman with a big, red nose, she was given her start by her cousin Sarah Jennings (duchess of Marlborough), who secured Abigail's appointment as bedchamber woman. Her devotion led to 'Abigail' becoming a type-name for a serving-woman. The Queen was present at her marriage in 1707 to Samuel Masham, 1st Baron Masham. By then her attentive, compliant service has led her to replace the domineering Sarah in the Queen's favour. Despite furious efforts by the Duchess to retain her place she was dismissed in 1711. Then a twist to the story: Abigail favoured James Stuart, rather than George I, and she retired to obscurity in Essex.
Buried **High Laver.**

MEAD, Isaac (1859-1922), farmer and author. Son of a farm labourer, crippled when young, Mead wrote farming articles, corresponded with ministers, including Winston Churchill. He campaigned successfully for the de-rating of agricultural land to help farm labourers and celebrated victory by setting a chapel window in his barn at Hornet's Farm. Wrote *Life of an Essex Lad* published in 1923, partly autobiographical, describing rural life in the Essex he knew in his early years.
In Hornet's Farm, now much changed, on the road to **Beauchamp Roding,** Mead made a garden tomb, consecrated, with a stone pillar bearing his wife's name; left a space for his own name, but it was never filled. Mead, his wife and family are all buried there.

MORANT, Rev Phillip (1700-70), antiquarian. Produced the 'only large-scale, complete and original history of Essex', according to Jarvis *View,* the result of enormous personal research as well as collecting and editing earlier material. Morant was inspired to historical work while a curate at Great Waltham under learned Dr Nicholas Tindal. Morant was born in Jersey, but lived in England from his school days. He impressed the Bishop of London by his religious writings and was given a series of Essex livings. Married Anne Stebbing of Great Tey in 1739. In 1745 rector of **Aldham,** where he was

buried. the tombstone from the old churchyard was
brought to the church in 1966 by the Essex Archaeological Society.

MORLEY, John (1656-1735), property dealer. Lucky to
have wealthy and influential Robert Harley, 1st earl of
Oxford, as patron. Introduced by Harley to the poet
Matthew Prior and, more importantly, to Alexander
Pope. He built up a prosperous business in Halstead as
a butcher, then amassed money by deals in property.
Remained modest, except for getting Kneller to paint
his portrait in 1716 and for having a family vault made
for himself in the Bourchier Chapel, **Halstead.** Morley's
tomb subsequently moved outside.
*Flint church, 14th-15th century. In the neighbourhood is
an 18th century weatherboarded mill of three storeys.*

*MUNNINGS, Sir Alfred (1878-1959), artist. President
of the Royal Academy, 1944-9. Famous for paintings of
horses and for controversial views on modern art. A
great conversationalist. Munnings lived at Castle House,
Dedham, where his last studio may sometimes be
visited.
*Pevsner considered Dedham 'easily the most attractive
small town in Essex', echoing Constable's love of the
place.
Buried at Dedham is Edmund Sherman, ancestor of
General Sherman of American Civil War fame. Edmund's
cousin Samuel emigrated to Massachusetts in 1634 and
settled in Contentment, later renamed Dedham.*

MYDDLETON, Sir Thomas (1550-1631), merchant. Born
at Denbigh Castle while his father was governor. In
1630 Myddleton arranged, at great expense, the first
popular edition of the Bible in Welsh. Very successful
in business, thanks partly to Sir Francis Walsingham,
Elizabeth I's minister. Myddleton a member of the
Grocer's Company, a surveyor of customs, charter
member of the East India Company, 1600, member of
the Virgina Company, 1623. Lord Mayor of London
1613, when his namesake, the playwright Thomas
Middleton, devised two pageants. Bought Stansted

Mountfitchet manor in 1615.

Myddleton's altar tomb at **Stansted Mountfitchet** one of the finest of its type in England. His daughter, Hester Salisbury, has another notable tomb.

The church has Norman doorways and chancel arch and a 17th century brick tower. A brick tower mill of 1787 still has its machinery.

NASSAU, William Henry de, 4th earl of Rochford (died 1781), statesman. Vice-Admiral of the Coasts of Essex 1748, later Lord-Lieutenant of county. Held many offices under George II and George III. Sent as envoy to Sardinia in 1749, ambassador to France in 1763 and to Vienna in 1768. Secretary of State to George III in 1776. Twice entertained George III at St Osyth Priory, where Nassau is said to have planted some of the earliest Lombardy poplars in England. A bastard son of a Prince of Orange and cousin to William III brought this branch of the family to England.

Monument in **St Osyth's** early 12th century church; here 16th century brick arcades separate nave from aisles.

NELSON, Horatio - see Scott.

NOEL, Rev. Conrad [le Despenser Roden] (1869-1942), vicar of Thaxted from 1910. Presented to the living by the socialist Countess of Warwick. Noel also a socialist; the novel *The Flag*, by Robert Shaw recounts the controversy aroused when Noel hoisted the Sinn Fein flag and the Red Flag, which Cambridge undergraduates tore down, provoking reprisals. Noel was active in journalism, had done pastoral work in London and Portsmouth slums, was arrested in Manchester for insisting on free speech. At Thaxted Noel transformed the church into a thoroughly appropriate setting for the moving services he conducted, helped in the church music by Gustav Holst, a resident in the town. Noel's wife, Miriam, inspired Thaxted revival of Morris dancing.

His tombstone at **Thaxted** is inscribed: 'He loved justice and hated oppression'. Bust in church.

Also in church are the royal arms of Queen Anne and a splendid 15th century pinnacled cover which completely encases the font. Thaxted Guildhall, 16th century, incorporates an old lock-up; the building timbered like others in the town, though some of the old buildings are plastered.

NUGENT, Robert, Earl Nugent (1702-88), politician and poet. A big, rollicking, brazen-voiced, high-spirited Irishman, Nugent was mocked in his day for marrying successively three widows who each brought him wealth, but no other happiness. The second wife, Anne (nee Coggs), was a 'fat and ugly dame', according to the generally restrained *D.N.B.* She brought him Gosfield, where Nugent made an extensive park. Oliver Goldsmith was a friend, while Nugent befriended the miserable Prince of Wales, son of George II, and advanced generous loans. The Prince didn't repay them, but George III did, with 'places, pensions and peerages'. Though Nugent was born a Roman Catholic, his celebrated poem 'Ode to William Pulteney' described how he passed to a 'purer faith'. Unfortunately it speedily appeared that Nugent had not written the ode, but had bought it. He died a Catholic.
Buried **Gosfield.**

*OATES, Captain Lawrence Edward Grace (1880-1912), soldier and explorer. Returned safely from the Boer War, so in gratitude one of the old church bells was recast at the little village of Gestingthorpe, where the family had the Hall. Oates served with the Inniskilling Dragoons. He was, of course, the 'very gallant gentleman' who, disabled, on his birthday, 17th March, 1912, walked out of the tent into an Antarctic blizzard, saying "I am going out now, and I may be some time." His vain hope was that his sacrifice would increase the chances of survival of the other members of the group on Captain Scott's ill-fated expedition to the South Pole.
A brass tablet in **Gestingthorpe** church, which has a brick tower and a double hammerbeam roof inside.

OGLETHORPE, James (1696-1785), founder of Georgia, U.S.A. Oglethorpe wanted to help prisoners, especially

debtors, and thought that settling them overseas was an improvement. Began by settling Savannah in 1732. Little trouble from Indians after signing a treaty with them; one chief accompanied him to England to be presented at Court. Oglethorpe had to fight the Spanish, whom he defeated, but it cost him all he had. Still, now a General, he returned to Britain in 1743 and married heiress Elizabeth Wright, whose fortune included Cranham Hall, near Upminster. Unfortunately intriguers got him court-martialled; fortunately, he was acquitted. He then gave up the army and turned squire.
Buried **Cranham** Church, near the Hall. Request from Oglethorpe University at Atlanta, Georgia, in 1925 for the transfer of his remains was turned down only after high-level consultations.

OSYTH, Saint (martyred 653). Daughter of the first Christian king of the East Angles and grand-daughter of pagan King Penda of Mercia. Taken to Warwickshire as a child for safe keeping. Betrothed to the king of the East Saxons, but the wedding was interrupted to hunt for a mysterious white stag. Osyth took the veil, was forgiven and granted the village of Chich, so that she could build a nunnery. It was raided by Danes and Osyth, refusing to abandon Christianity, was beheaded, only for her to pick up her head and carry it to the nearby church door. The Danes were unmanned and fled. A spring of water arose as she was killed and is still flowing in Nun's Wood. **Saint Osyth** buried in church on the site of the present St Peter & St Paul. Her shrine became famous for miracles and thus a centre for pilgrimage.
The nunnery became a priory, the splendid 15th century gatehouse still being extant, three-storeyed, battlemented, and patterned in flint and stone. A Martello Tower built at St Osyth during the Napoleonic Wars; two others in the vicinity.

PARKER, William, Baron Morley and Lord Mounteagle (1575-1622), revealed Gunpowder Plot. A Catholic, he joined Catesby and others in Essex's rebellion, 1601; released from Tower on payment of £8,000. Became

less extreme as a favourite of James I, even willing to
recant. On 26th October, 1605, at a supper he was
giving, Mounteagle was warned by letter not to attend
Parliament on 5th November. He took the letter to
Whitehall, and attended the search of Parliament by
Suffolk, lord chamberlain. The conspirators arrested. It
is thought that Lady Mounteagle's brother, Francis
Tresham, wrote the letter, assuming - like Mounteagle
- that the conspirators knew the plot was to be
exposed in time for them to escape.
Mounteagle buried in **Great Hallingbury.**
*Roman bricks in church fabric, early Norman chancel
arch.*

PAYCOCK, Thomas (died 1518), clothier. In *King John*,
Shakespeare used Abbot Ralph de Coggeshall's story of
Hubert de Burgh and little Prince Arthur (John's
nephew). Most visitors to Coggeshall go to admire the
beautiful timbered, panelled and ornamented house,
Paycock's. Perhaps it was John Paycock, butcher, who
built the house (c.1500) for his son Thomas as a
wedding present when marrying Margaret Horrold.
Initials T.P. are on the frieze. The family mark was an
ermine tail. Thomas is buried in St Katherine's Church,
Coggeshall, where there is a Paycock Chapel, much
damaged by a marauding German plane in September,
1940, now restored. Another Thomas Paycock lived in
what was later called the Fleece Inn and has a brass in
the family chapel.
*Wool Pack Inn, 15th century, gabled, among other
interesting buildings.*

PERRERS, Alice (died 1400), mistress of Edward III.
Not beautiful in face or figure, but held on to Edward
and power by her honeyed words. She interfered with
justice for her own ends and for those who bribed her
most. John of Gaunt gave her 'a harrap of beryl
garnished with silver gilt'. The King gave her manors in
Upminster. As he lay dying she is supposed to have
pulled the rings from his fingers. Twice banished, but
returned, and she prospered afresh after marrying
William de Windsor, formerly deputy of Ireland; he died
in debt to the crown, 1384.

Buried, as she directed 'before the altar of Our Lady the Virgin' in **Upminster** church.

PETRE, Sir William (c.1505-72), statesman. Devon-born founder of the great Essex family. Chancellor of the Order of the Garter. Served Henry VIII, Edward VI, and Mary as Secretary of State, retaining influence under Elizabeth I. Visitor of Monasteries for Thomas Cromwell and acquired land at Ingatestone. He built Ingatestone Hall, where John Payne, the only priest to be executed in Essex under Elizabeth, was betrayed by the apostate George Elliott, later betrayer of Edmund Campion. The Hall is still owned by the family, but part is leased to Essex County Council for exhibitions. Among permanent displays in the Long Gallery is a rare 16th century virginal, a reminder that the composer William Byrd frequently visited the house.
Petre buried **Ingatestone** with imposing monument.
The 15th century diapered brick west tower of the church is widely regarded as the finest in Essex.

POYNTZ, Sir Gabriel (died 1608). High Sheriff 1577 and 1589. Knighted 1604. Same family as Poins in Shakespeare's *Henry IV*.
Buried **North Ockendon:** notable tomb. As Addison notes, Sir Gabriel saw that several members of the family were suitably commemorated. Most interesting was Thomas Poyntz, a London merchant in Antwerp, who befriended William Tyndale, translator of the Bible, and was therefore condemned to be burned like Tyndale, but escaped; succeeded his brother John at North Ockendon.

RADCLIFFE, James, 3rd earl of Derwentwater (1689-1716), Jacobite. Handsome and romantic, but fatally rash. Brought up in France with Jacobite exiles at the court of St Germain. The rashness was in deciding to turn out in the '15. Captured and executed. His brother Charles, 2nd earl, turned out in the '45 and was likewise executed.
In 1874 the bodies were brought for reinterment in the Roman Catholic Chapel of Thordon Hall, **Ingrave.**

Ingrave church, 18th century, of red brick, is among the best of the period in Essex.

RADCLIFFE, Thomas, 3rd earl of Sussex (1526?-83), courtier and soldier. Turned from supporting Lady Jane Grey to supporting Mary, whose marriage to Philip II of Spain he helped to arrange. As Lord Deputy of Ireland, Sussex failed to defeat Shane O'Neill and also failed to capture the Earls of Westmorland and Northumberland despite invading Scotland in pursuit. He had rivalry with the Earl of Leicester, to thwart whom he advocated Elizabeth I's marriage to Archduke Charles, later to the Duc d'Alencon; he seemed to be succeeding, but fell ill, so failed yet again. His second wife was Frances, aunt of Sir Philip Sidney, who died 1558, leaving £5,000 for the foundation of Sidney Sussex College, Cambridge. Sussex buried **Boreham** (alabaster effigy) with parents and grandparents, at their feet monkeys wearing hats.

RAY, John (1627-1705), 'the greatest of all field naturalists' (Charles Raven, Ray's biographer). Cuvier said that Ray had laid the foundations of the science of zoology, by methodical classification of 11,000 plants. Ray received £5 profit on the three volumes. He lectured on Greek and mathematics at Cambridge until he was driven out for sectarian reasons. He explored England, Scotland and Wales, collecting natural history specimens, describing and cataloguing them. He continued these activities on the continent with pupils. He had wide interests, from rare words and phrases surviving in English to musk-scented insects, the air-bladder of fish and the anatomy of porpoises. There is a school at Braintree named after him.
Ray was buried at **Black Notley,** where he was born, son of the village blacksmith.
The church has a typical Essex shingled broached spire. Hall has big 15th century barn.

RICH (née Boyle), Mary, Countess of Warwick (1625-78), Puritan votaress. The sister of Robert Boyle, chemist and physicist of Boyle's Law. At 15 she married Charles Rich, later 4th earl of Warwick. When her young son was ill she swore to change her life if he recovered and, after he did, she turned devout Puritan. At Leighs Priory she prayed and meditated in her favourite wooded spot called the Sanctuary. Puritan clergy were welcomed to the Priory, even if they had been ejected from their livings. The Countess wrote a diary and an autobiography of some historic interest, while her *Occasional meditations* have spontaneity and simple charm. She had need of solace for her husband was unbearably irritable from gout and the stone. Both Aubrey and Horace Walpole spoke well of the Countess. She was buried at **Felsted.**

Leighs Priory, founded about 1220, was dismantled by Richard Rich (q.v.), who built a large house on the site. Much of the outer courtyard remains, as do two gatehouses of patterned vitrified brick, and elaborate chimneystacks. Like Thomas Audley (q.v.), the Rich family had as their motto 'Garde ta Foy'.

RICH, Richard, 1st Baron Rich (1496-1566?), Lord Chancellor. Among his good deeds he founded Felsted Grammar School (attended by Cromwell's sons, of whom Richard died at 18 and was buried in the church there); he endowed almshouses; and gave herrings to the local poor. He could afford to as he had been awarded 20 manors in Essex alone for his work in transferring church property to Henry VIII after the Dissolution. On the debit side he betrayed a long list of people (some his friends) from Sir Thomas More, Thomas Cromwell and Thomas Wriothesley (with whom he racked poor Anne Askew in the Tower) to Protector Somerset and Lady Jane Grey. Active in persecuting Catholics, then Essex Puritans, notably at Bocking.
Buried **Felsted,** recumbent under a carved canopy and a 15ft monument of marble and alabaster, sculpted by Epiphanius Evesham. His son was 'the Rich fool' who married Penelope Devereux, the Stella of Sir Philip Sidney.

RICH, Robert, 2nd earl of Warwick (1587-1658), Puritan leader. Rich did much to colonise the Bermudas and settle New England. At home he led the Puritan party in Essex. He opposed Ship Money and raised Parliamentary troops. The Long Parliament made him Lord High

Admiral. He was successively Lord-Lieutenant of Essex, Captain General of London and the neighbouring counties and Speaker of the House of Lords. His wife, the Countess, and his steward held off a Royalist attack on Leighs (Leez) Priory under Lord Goring and Sir Charles Lucas.
Buried **Felsted.**
Church is one of those with an 18th century cupola on a Norman tower.

ROE, Sir Thomas (c.1580-1644), diplomat. Very active and very skilful. A friend of Ben Jonson and Raleigh (even when Raleigh was in disgrace). A political agent in the West Indies and South America, being the first European to penetrate 300 miles up the Amazon. The Ambassador (expenses paid by the East India Company), 1615-18, to the Great Mogul in Agra: his journals reprinted 1899 from Purchas and other sources. He returned home through Persia. The Ambassador to the Ottoman Porte, 1621-8, active in benefiting English trade, liberating slaves, acquiring Biblical manuscript, the Codex Alexandrinus. Roe advised Elizabeth, the 'Winter Queen' of Bohemia, and Gustavus Adolphus of Sweden and otherwise promoted the Protestant cause in the Thirty Years War. Ambassador extraordinary to Regensburg (then Ratisbon) in Bavaria.
Buried **Woodford.**

RUGGLES-BRISE, Sir Evelyn John (1857-1935), penal reformer. Chairman of the Prison Commission, 1895-1921, sought to improve the treatment of young offenders, introduced the Borstal system of training in 1901 (Borstal, near Rochester). Like William Kempe earlier, he owned Spains Hall, a 16th century house of red brick, dressed with stone, its porch two-storeyed, its front having seven gables.
Buried **Finchingfield.** Memorial tablet: 'through his vision and persistence he saved the young from a life of crime'.

SALTER, John Henry (1841-1930), physician and diarist.

RESTING PLACES - ESSEX

Salter might have gone far in medicine, but the loss of
an eye limited him to general practice, though he made
himself an authority on diphtheria. For 60 years in
Tolleshunt D'Arcy, where he kept a diary of absorbing
interest. In his lifetime very popular and esteemed.
Despite his handicap, Salter maintained an interest in
sport, from shooting and boxing to horses (riding and
racing) and dogs, especially coursing. Asked several
times to judge dog shows in Russia, where he shot a
bear now in Chelmsford & Essex Museum. Some of his
dogs were ordered by the King of Sweden.
Salter was buried at **Tolleshunt D'Arcy.**
Before 1800 the apple D'Arcy Spice (known by other
names, including Baddow Pippin) was grown in the
garden of Tolleshunt D'Arcy Hall and, by mid-19th
century, had been recognised as a variety for
cultivation.

SANDYS, Cecily Wilford (died 1619), wife of Edwin
Sandys (1516-88), archbishop of York. Her story has
been overshadowed by her Puritan husband's (details in
Addison, *Worthies*). Sandys was one of the translators
of the Bishops' Bible and he suppoted Lady Jane Grey,
as a staunch Protestant rather than as a believer in her
right to succeed, but he considered it his duty to
proclaim Mary Tudor at Cambridge. Imprisoned in the
Tower, 1553, later released and fled to Europe where
his first wife and child died. He returned to England
and married Cecily in 1559. Sandys flourished for a
time under Elizabeth, but in 1581 was the victim of a
frame-up at Doncaster, where a naked woman was paid
to force herself on him and he was terrified into
paying blackmail; eventually he plucked up the courage
to report the incident to Burghley and the Queen and
was acquited at a Star Chamber trial, though the
villain, Sir Robert Stapleton, hounded Sandys afterwards.
Cecily Sandys has a great monument in **Woodham
Ferrers** church, a place where the Archbishop had
connections.
A small nature reserve is nearby.

*SAYERS, Dorothy L[eigh] (1893-1957), author. Lived

for a time in Newland Street, |**Witham,** as the names
of several modern developments remind us: Dorothy
Sayers Drive, also Wimsey Court, after her detective
hero, and Vane Court, after Wimsey's beloved. See
Norfolk entry.
*Witham has many old houses, some Georgian, some even
more venerable, and the restored Spread Eagle Inn is
particularly delightful. Good flint church of St Nicholas,
14th century; Chipping Hill very pleasant, where ancient
houses surround a little triangular green.*

*SCOTT, Rev Alexander John (1768-1840), naval
chaplain. he attended the dying Nelson in *Victory*   and
brought the ship's chart table, a ~~bureau and a mirror~~
to the vestry of St Leonard's church, **Southminster,**
where Scott was vicar 1809-40. Scott served by private
arrangement as Nelson's private secretary and interpreter in the Mediterranean 1803-5, going ashore at
various ports to gather intelligence. The Admiralty
regarded these trips as leave and stopped Scott's pay as
chaplain for such periods. Before Southminster, Scott
was curate at Burnham-on-Crouch.

SCROGGS, Sir William (c.1630-83), judge. In the mould
of Judge Jeffreys. At the trial following Titus Oates'
'Popish plot', Scroggs combined roles of judge and
prosecutor and condemned innocent people. Opinion was
so outraged that he took fright, acquitting some of the
guiltless and turning on Titus Oates. Still wildly unpopular, Charles II retired him (with a pension of
£1,500). Sir Walter Scott wrote of Scroggs after his
failure of nerve in *Peveril of the Peak.*
Scroggs buried **South Weald.**

SHILLIBEER, George (1797-1866), pioneer of omnibus
services. First built an omnibus in Paris, where he was
a coach-builder. In 1829 he started a service with two
horse-drawn buses from Paddington to the Bank of
England at one shilling a head (the stage coach charged
half a crown) and supplied free newspapers and
magazines. Extended his London services, but was no
businessman and had to change his service in 1834 to
one from London to Greenwich and Woolwich. Railway

competition ruined him and he turned from buses. He ended as an undertaker in City Road, introducing a patent funeral coach and reducing the cost of funerals. Buried in **Chigwell** churchyard. In the centenary year, 1929, London busmen presented a plaque to the church for the founder of their occupation.

SMITH, Rodney ('Gipsy') (1860-1947), evangelist. Born in a gipsy caravan, hence his nickname, in Waltham Forest. Religious conversion in his teens after attending a Primitive Methodist meeting. Joined the Salvation Army early on, but decided to leave in 1882 for a personal crusade of evangelism, which eventually took him round the world. Death came on a transatlantic liner. Buried, at his own request, in **Epping Forest.** After a memorial service in 1978 his grave was marked by a stone.

STAPLE, Thomas (died 1371), sergeant at arms to Edward III. Humbly born, judging by the staples in his heraldic arms. Buried **Shopland** in tomb chest, but the church was destroyed in 1958. Only the top half of Staples' brass effigy was left and it was taken to nearby **Sutton** church and placed on the wall. There also remained the lid of the tomb and this too was taken to Sutton churchyard. Some years ago Mr George D Kissell was among those who arranged for the stone to be brought into the church and for the brass to be laid on it.

STORRS, Sir Ronald Henry Amherst (1881-1955), Near Eastern expert and governor. Admired by Lawrence of Arabia for urbanity and artfulness, Storrs had many interests, from the arts and literature to cooking and conversation, which he consciously shaped into a craft. He would mix with anyone whose company he deemed worthwhile. He had a gift for collecting *objets d'art* in unlikely places. Ten years' service in Egypt, during which he collaborated with Lord Kitchener. Negotiations in 1914 with Sharif Husain led to meeting with T E Lawrence. He was Governor of Jerusalem in 1917 and Governor of Cyprus in 1926; Government House there burnt down in 1931 destroying his books and works of

art. Governor of Northern Rhodesia, 1932-4. Wrote the absorbing and stimulating *Orientations*, 1937.
Buried **Pebmarsh.**

STRUTT, John William, 3rd Lord Rayleigh (1842-1919), scientist. Awarded the Nobel Prize for physics in 1904, he gave the money to extending the Cavendish Laboratory, Cambridge.He discovered a new gas, argon, with his friend Sir William Ramsay. A great authority on physical optics, he suggested that the sky is blue because dust particles in the air scatter the shorter waves of light. Author of nearly 450 scientific papers. He calculated the amount of milk needed for the expanding population of London and started a cattle herd on the family farm at Terling, opening eight dairy shops in London. Chancellor of Cambridge University, President of the Royal Society and of the British Association, Privy Councillor, Order of Merit (one of the original twelve). Retired to Terling in 1885 for work in his private laboratory.
Buried **Terling.**
Church has a tower of 1732. Smock mill was working until a generation ago.

STUKELEY, Rev. William (1687-1765), physician and antiquary. Described as 'a strange compound of simplicity, drollery, absurdity, superstition and antiquarianism'. A Druid enthusiast. For Stukeley Druidism was 'the aboriginal patriarchal religion', Stonehenge was a Druid work; he had a 'Druid temple' in his Grantham garden. For him freemasonry was 'the remains of the mysterys of the antients', hence he became a mason. He took orders in 1729; once postponed his service so the congregation could watch an eclipse of the sun. At 75 he found he needed spectacles and, when he got them, he preached from the text 'Now we see through a glass darkly'. He undertook long rides, despite his gout, seeking antiquities and collected coins, fossils and pictures. In particular he visited Stonehenge on several occasions and studied the monuments. By modern standards he was an unsatisfactory field-worker, and he was wrong-headed, but Stukeley's enthusiasm greatly invigorated archaeology. There is a biography by Stuart

Piggott, recently republished, enlarged and revised.
Stukeley buried at St Mary Magdalene Church, High
Street South, **East Ham.**

TAYLOR, Jane (1783-1824), writer for children. The
whole family wrote, and some painted, engraved or
invented. Francis Galton claimed them as examples of
diffusion of hereditary talent. Jane was precocious,
writing from the age of eight, alone or with sister Ann.
Together with their father they produced the very
popular *Original Poems for Infant Minds,* 1805, which
includes 'My Mother', by Ann, who later wrote
'Meddlesome Matty'. More poems followed, notably
'Twinkle, twinkle little star', by Jane. Her verse was
admired by Scott, her prose by Browning. The sisters
weren't always encouraged by their parents. The family
lived at Lavenham, 1786-96 (see Suffolk entry, Spring).
Jane Taylor buried in ground attached to the Congregational Chapel, **Chipping Ongar.**
*David Livingstone trained here as Congregational
missionary, 1838-9.*
*Edward Boodle, founder of Boodle's Club, was also
buried at Ongar.*
*Chipping Ongar still has the mound of a Norman castle
and also a much altered Norman church. The Corner
Shop of 1642 is opposite the King's Head of 1697.*

THORNE, William James (Will) (1857-1946), Labour
pioneer. Born in Birmingham, had no formal education,
since he began working 10½ hours a day for 2s.6d a
week when aged 6. No wonder, therefore, that at first
marriage in 1879 Thorne couldn't sign his own name.
With Ben Tillett in 1889 he started the National Union
of Gasworkers and General Labourers, ancestor of the
powerful General & Municipal Workers' Union. Thorne
was a West Ham councillor in 1890, MP for West Ham
South in 1895, retaining his seat after the constituency
was divided. In 1917, as Mayor of West Ham, he showed
George V how the poor lived. A big, strong man, no
parliamentarian, but devoted to the Labour movement,
the union and his constituency.
Buried in his constituency in the **East London** cemetery,
not far from Upton Manor where he died.

WAAD, Sir William (1546-1623), diplomatist. Son, according to himself, of the 'English Columbus', Armigel Waad (died 1568) 'the first Englishman to discover America'. Both claims wrong, though Armigel did sail to Cape Breton and Newfoundland in 1536 and home by a route so far north that he saw icebergs in midsummer. Armigel Waad served Henry VIII when he got back, but Mary dismissed him. Elizabeth compensated him and sent him on a mission to the Duke of Holstein in 1559.

Despite being wrong about his father, the son, Sir William, had a most interesting life, too interesting for comfort at times. He was deep in politics and the intrigues of the period. A secret agent on the continent for Lord Burghley. Ambassador to Portugal, 1580; on return made secretary to Walsingham, the head of Elizabeth's intelligence service, for whom Waad carried out many missions. Paid £30 for seizing Mary Stuart papers, implicating her in the Babington Plot, 1586. As clerk of the Privy Council Waad was zealous in sniffing out treasonable practices. With others he bought the Bermudas from the Virginia Company and resigned them to the crown. Knighted by James I, appointed Lieutenant of the Tower, 1605: dismissed 1613 on the pretext (false) of inadequately guarding Arabella Stuart and embezzling her jewels; really because he guarded Sir Thomas Overbury so closely that the wicked Frances Howard, Countess of Essex, couldn't get at him: within weeks of Waad's dismissal Overbury was found poisoned. Waad encouraged many writers, from John Taylor, the Water Poet, to Hooker of *Ecclesiastical Polity*.

Waad built Battails Hall, **Munden,** the place where he is buried. His memorial in a large church with a brick floor also celebrates Armigel Waad.

WALDEGRAVE, Sir Edward (1517-61), politican. Loyal and devout Roman Catholic, for which he suffered much. In the household of Princess (afterwards Queen) Mary under Edward VI. The Privy Council forbad her to celebrate mass at Copt Hall, Epping, but none of her household dared insist, so great was her indignation: Waldegrave and others sent to the Tower for not

insisting. Elizabeth I deprived him of office and he retired to Borley. Charged with permitting mass, would not take the Oath of Supremacy, so to the Tower again. He died there.
There is a six-poster tomb in **Borley** church.

WALDEGRAVE, James, 1st earl Waldegrave (1685-1741), diplomatist. His grandmother was James II's eldest daughter; Waldegrave's father made Baron by James and took money to Paris for him. Waldegrave educated in France, married a Catholic lady, then turned Protestant, to the alarm of his uncle, the Duke of Berwick, and other Jacobites. Robert Walpole found much diplomatic work for Waldegrave, who was very good at it; his last appointment was to Versailles (where he controlled English secret agents in France). He built Navestock Hall (pulled down 1811).
Buried in the chancel of **Navestock** church, which has a spire above the belfry. Waldegrave's daughter-in-law, subsequently Duchess of Gloucester (see below) erected monument to him.

WALDEGRAVE, James, 2nd earl Waldegrave (1715-63), reluctantly Prime Minister for five days in 1757. Son of above. Adviser and friend to George II, keeper of the privy purse to the Prince of Wales. When ousted, he intrigued to part Pitt and Fox. Horace Walpole success-fully urged him to marry Maria, natural daughter of Sir Edward Walpole, 'the handsomest woman in England', half his age. Reynolds painted her several times. She survived until 1807, turned down the Duke of Portland and married George III's favourite brother, the Duke of Gloucester, at a secret ceremony because of the King's disapproval. Outlived Gloucester too.
2nd earl buried **Navestock,** like his father.

WARNER, Richard (1711-75), botanist. A banker's son. Lawyer in Woodford Green, but his chief interest was in his botanical garden where he concentrated on rare plants. Studied local flora, writing *Plantae Woodfordien-sis.* Knew Linnaeus and became a friend of Hogarth and Garrick, the latter perhaps because Warner trans-lated the zestful, sometimes coarse Latin comedies of

Plautus, from whom Shakespeare derived his *Comedy of Errors* and Moliere his miser, *L'Avare.*
Warner buried **Woodford** churchyard in altar tomb.

WASHINGTON, Rev. Laurence (1602-52), last direct English ancestor (great-great-grandfather) of George Washington. For ten years rector of Purleigh, ejected 1643 as a Royalist. Became curate at Little Braxted, then to Maldon. Son John who, like a brother, emigrated to America, became George's great-grandfather.
Laurence buried St Peter's Church, **Maldon.** Memorial window to Laurence in All Saints, Maldon, 1928. Purleigh was given a painting of George Washington's mother by W Lanier Washington.
Only the tower of St Peter's extant, but the register exists, with a record of the christening of Christopher Jones, captain of the Mayflower.

WESTERN, Charles Callis, Baron Western (1767-1844), agriculturist and politician. A man of wide interests, who collected antiquarian objects, especially marble, on extensive travels. Advocated agricultural reform and himself responsible for progress in sheep-breeding. An amateur economist. Wrote on prison discipline. MP for Maldon 1790-1812, then for Essex 1812-32. Housed his collection at Felix Hall, Rivenhall.
Monument in **Rivenhall** Church, which was practically rebuilt in 1838 and has, perhaps, the finest medieval stained glass in Essex, some 12th century, brought from Sarthe in France for the east window.

WILBYE, John (1574-1638), madrigalist. Widely considered the greatest English madrigal composer, mostly on the strength of two sets, 1598 and 1609, for he published little and few manuscript compositions of his are preserved. Son of a Norfolk tanner, Wilbye's obvious talent gained him the patronage of the Cornwallis family of Suffolk. A Cornwallis daughter married Sir Thomas Kytson of Hengrave Hall and from 1594 to 1628 Wilbye served the Kytson family, who furthered his career. At Hengrave a good collection of musical instruments was available, some possibly for hired per-

formers, but most for Kytson retainers. Wilbye spent his last ten years in Colchester (there is a plaque on a house in Trinity Street that belonged to Sir Thomas Kytson's younger daughter, Countess Rivers).
Wilbye buried Holy Trinity Church, **Colchester.**

WILLINGALE family. Commoners at Loughton. See *Portrait of Epping Forest* by Sir William Addison for details of the Willingales' fight for the freedom of Epping Forest in the mid-19th century. Enclosures and sale of crown rights threatened villagers' livelihood. Thomas Willingale and his nephew Alfred (1843-1913) challenged the squire of Loughton over the legality of closures and were much aided by Sir Thomas Fowell Buxton, a reformer like his grandfather (see Norfolk). The Maitland family of esquires lived at Loughton Hall until it was destroyed by fire, as recounted in *Barnaby*
            Fascinating particulars in Addison include an account of Thomas Willingale's son, Samuel William (1840-1911), a strange brooding figure, who kept two adders in a long stocking down the leg of his trousers after he had drawn their poison by goading them to attack a red handkerchief hung over a fence.
Thomas Willingale buried in family grave in St Nicholas's churchyard, **Loughton.** Samuel William said to be buried in St John's churchyard, Loughton.

WINSTANLEY, William (c.1627-98), almanac compiler. A fervent Royalist, Winstanley said Milton's 'fame is gone out like a candle in a snuff and his memory will always stink'. Winstanley's own verse is now regarded as doggerel. He started as a London barber and is thus called the Barber Poet, but abandoned the razor to use the scissors for making up his *Poor Robin's Almanacs,* popular in his day. He also sold chapbooks.
Buried **Quendon.** So, according to some, was his brother Thomas - in wool, as prescribed by law for a time. Others say that Thomas was buried at St Mary's Church, Saffron Walden.
Thomas's son, Henry Winstanley, built the first Eddystone Lighthouse and was killed in the storm that destroyed it in 1703.

Quendon church was rebuilt 1861; given a new bell-cote in 1963, a landmark for miles.

WISEMAN, John (died 1558), an Auditor to Henry VIII. A Roman Catholic. Knighted at the Battle of the Spurs, 1513. Details of the family in Addison, *Worthies*.   In Wiseman house at Wimbush, Fathers Garnett and Gerard were concealed in 1592 and got away.
Buried (with brass) at **Great Canfield,** a church in a fine setting with 13th century mural of Virgin and Child.
Great mound, 45ft high and 275 ft across, of de Vere motte and bailey castle.

WITHERINGS, Thomas (died 1651), 'founder of the Post Office'. In 1633 appointed postmaster for letters abroad. He found the whole system inefficient and set about making it reliable; soon succeeded. In addition to this achievement, Witherings was also responsible for establishing a registered-letter service.
Memorial in St Andrew's Church, **Hornchurch,** whose copper-covered spire rises 120 feet above the tower.
Over east end of chancel a rebus of a bull's head in stone and copper.

WOOD, Sir Henry Evelyn (1838-1919), soldier and administrator. Joined Navy and fought ashore with the Naval Brigade in the Crimean War. Transferred to Army, winning the Victoria Cross in the aftermath of the Indian Mutiny. After service in Africa became the first British sirdar of the Egyptian army. As administrator at the War Office improved transport of troops. Keen foxhunter.
Buried **Cressing.**
Cressing was the earliest English possession (1135) of the Knights Templars. The Manor became a private farm early in the 16th century and has two remarkable timber-framed barns, with whole oak trees used as main posts. Barley barn, c.1450, weatherboarded; larger wheat barn (140 ft long and 40 ft high), c.1530, is brick-nogged (bricks between the timbers).

WOODLEY, Hester (1705?-67), slave. Like other Negro slaves in those days she was given the surname of her mistress (Mrs Bridget Woodley). On the lady's death, her daughter, not unnaturally, got her mother's belongings, the slave included.

Hester is buried outside the porch of the modern church at **Little Parndon,** Harlow.

Holy Cross, Felsted [see pages 67 and 68]

Norfolk

*ATKYNS (née Walpole), Lady Charlotte (1756-1836), friend of Marie Antoinette. Involved in Scarlet Pimpernel-type, though unsuccessful, adventures during the French Revolution. Daringly tried several times to rescue Marie Antoinette from Temple jail. After the Queen's execution, Charlotte devoted her fortune to plans for arranging the escape of the Dauphin, again in vain. She had been an actress at Sheridan's Drury Lane Theatre, then went to Versailles and met Marie Antoinette after marrying Edward Atkyns of Ketteringham Hall, near Hethersett.
Died Paris (grave unknown). Memorial inscription in **Ketteringham** church, very attractive after restoration early in 19th century, Gothic style. Other Atkyns memorials there; also to Hevenyngham family, notably marble monument to Sir William Hevenyngham (died 1678), a judge at Charles I's trial who refused to sign the death warrant.

*BABES IN THE WOOD. Legend derived from a ballad has it that before dying in the 16th century Arthur Truelove of Griston charged their uncle with the care of his little son and daughter. The Uncle, however, was Wicked. He wanted their inheritance for himself and hired two men to kill the children. One man found himself unable to do so, quarrelled with his harder-hearted companion and slew him, but then left the childen to starve to death in Wayland (a corruption of Wailing?) Wood, near Watton. A robin covered the children with leaves and moss. The wood is said to be haunted by two little ghosts - the large airfield is sure to have disturbed their rest. The Elizabethan Griston Hall is sometimes claimed to have been Truelove's house, sometimes that of the Wicked Uncle. **Griston** church font has a quaint inscription recording restoration of the tower, 1568.

BEDINGFIELD, Sir Henry (1511-83). His father, Sir Edmund, was the reputedly harsh jailer of Catherine of Aragon at Kimbolton. Sir Henry, a staunch Catholic supporter, early rallied to Mary Tudor against Lady Jane Grey. Made jailer of Princess Elizabeth in the Tower and at Woodstock; he too was accused of harshness, but his strictness did ensure that she wasn't assassinated. As Queen, Elizabeth only discouraged Sir Henry from attending court.
Memorial, with others of family, in lovely Bedingfield Chapel, **Oxborough** church, founded 1513, an early English example of Renaissance work in terracotta. The Chapel survived the fall of the parish church spire in 1818; the spire rebuilt, but in 1948 it collapsed, along with the tower causing much damage, so the chancel had to be used as the church.
Sir Edmund began beautiful Oxburgh Hall - the house uses the shorter spelling - in 1482, of brick, moated, with a gatehouse probably the biggest of brick in England having an interior brick spiral staircase. Henry VIII occupied the King's Chamber in the Hall, and Mary,Queen of Scots, had the Queen's Chamber above it during her spell of imprisonment there. She occupied herself with needlework, many panels being incorporated in the Oxburgh Hangings. Elizabeth may have slept in the Queen's Chamber on her Norfolk Progress in 1578 during Sir Henry's lifetime. Near Hall is a Gothic Revival chapel by Pugin, 1835; medieval fittings.

BENDISH (née Ireton), Bridget (1650-1725), Oliver Cromwell's eccentric grand-daughter. Bridget married 1670, early widowed, worked husband's farm and salt pans at South Town, Yarmouth. After much food and drink and a short sleep, she liked to dress up to attend assembly in Yarmouth to return home singing a psalm or a hymn by Isaac Watts, a friend of hers. She would violently defend her grandfather's reputation and faith.

Allegedly involved in the Rye House Plot, 1685. No pension; no money sense.

Buried **Yarmouth.**

Still an interesting town, despite WWII bomb damage to its famous narrow streets, the Rows, and its decline as a fishing port and growth as a resort. Nelson column, 1817, comparable with Trafalgar Square's, but has Britannia on top. Birthplace of Anna Sewell at 26 Church Plain.

BLOGG, Henry George (1876-1954), coxswain of Cromer lifeboat for 38 years, serving with Cromer lifeboats for 53. During that service 873 lives were saved. Blogg three times awarded the gold medal of the Royal National Life-boat Institution. On the third occasion, in 1941, also given the British Empire medal for saving 88 men from six steamers in convoy; and in that year the George Cross. Four times awarded the RNLI's silver medal. In 1924 the Empire Gallantry Medal. He retired in 1947 and the next year the new Cromer lifeboat was named the *Henry Blogg*. No wonder there is a bust of him, looking out to sea, on the east cliff at Cromer. A quiet man, who did not smoke or drink, he was kindly and humorous with great qualities of personality and, of course, endurance. Strange that he was bullied at school; he was not fond of games, though a good pupil. He never learned to swim.

Buried at **Cromer.**

Cromer's church tower 'the tallest in Norfolk', at one period a lighthouse. Town's narrow high-walled streets were known to Jane Austen's Mr Woodhouse, who was enthusiastic. A favourite resort of Gurneys, Buxtons and many celebrities, visited by such as Oscar Wilde, and the Empress of Austria, Ellen Terry and Winston Churchill, Sir James Barrie and Kate Greenaway.

BLOMEFIELD, Rev. Francis (1705-52), historian. Discovered many unpublished Paston letters at Oxnead during his travels round the county for his history of Norfolk. Blomefield was never able to publish the letters. For long rector of Fersfield, where he set up his own printing press, destroyed by fire with the first

edition of his work. Many other troubles. Going to London for documents for the third (unfinished) volume of his history, he caught smallpox and died (in debt): he had refused inoculation as 'wrong to attempt to avoid evils sent by his Creator'. Blomefield's *History*, a labour of love, has been criticised by scholars.
Buried **Fersfield** in the chancel.
The 13th century church was mostly built by the de Bois family; a rare oak figure of Sir Robert de Bois (wood used because of his name?). His sister built the small tower, only 13 feet square.

*BOLEYN, Ann (1507-36). Accused of adultery and incest with her brother, George Boleyn, Viscount Rochford, and executed. Childhood at Blickling Hall.
1] Said to be buried at **Sall** church, one of the most beautiful in England.
Bequests from the Boleyn family, the Fountains and the Briggs. The roof spanning the nave is a remarkable building feat. Beautifully proportioned north and south porches, with chambers above; great bosses in the chancel roof depict the life of Christ. Seven-sacrament font cover suspended from ringers' gallery. Unfortunately the church became isolated after losing its congregation.
2]Ann Boleyn's heart reputedly discovered, 1836, in the south wall of the church of **Elveden Park,** near Thetford, and reburied near organ.

BROWNE, Sir Thomas (1605-82), physician and prose writer. '... obscure but gorgeous', Charles Lamb said of Browne's marvellous rhythmical and sonorous prose (Penguin edition in print). '... the iniquity of oblivion blindely scattereth her poppy' is a typical cadence, from the superb *Urn Buriall*, a meditation inspired by grave-goods unearthed at Old Walsingham. Speaking of the urns, Browne said 'Time which antiquates antiquities, and hath an art to make dust of all things, hath yet spared these minor Monuments'. After Oxford, Browne studied at continental universities; MD from Leyden c.1633. A man of enormous learning and curiosity, at once grave and whimsical, 'a crack'd Archangel', Herman Melville called him. Browne led an uneventful life. Knighted by Charles II at Norwich in 1671, the mayor having declined the honour.

Browne is buried in the splendid St Peter Mancroft Church, **Norwich,** dominating the Market Place; portrait by H Morland in vestry. Statue - with urn - close by in the Haymarket.

BURRAWAY, Christopher (died 1730), unwittingly guilty of incest. He married Alice, stated in the inscription on a slab under the tower of Martham church to have been 'in this life my sister, my mistress, my mother and my wife'. It came about in this way: Alice had an illegitimate son by her father. Unaware of his pedigree, Christopher left home, but returned in manhood, still ignorant, and found work as steward for Alice, who did not recognise him. He took her as mistress, presently married her and only then did the story come out, for Alice identified him by a mole on his body.

Both buried **Martham** church, near several Broads. So was St Blide, mother of St Walstan.

The church tower is notable; nave and chancel restored in Victorian Gothic, with 'inventive luxuriance of carving'. Village has a green and some 18th century houses, also the Countryside Collection, a museum of village life, with an aviary.

BUXTON, Sir Thomas Fowell, 1st baronet (1786-1845), social reformer. Shocked by conditions in East London, Buxton aided starving Spitalfields weavers. He married Hannah Gurney, sister of Elizabeth Fry, whom he assisted in prison work. Active in the Bible Society. Worked as MP for Weymouth, 1818-37, to amend criminal law. His greatest work was as an abolitionist and he succeeded Wilberforce in 1824 as anti-slavery leader; instrumental in the passage of the Abolition Act in 1835. He then campaigned against the African slave trade. Later interested in land improvement near Cromer amd other agricultural advances. Created a baronet in 1840.

Buried **Overstrand** in family burial ground at the east end of a neglected church.

CALTHORPE, Sir James. Of human, rather than historical, interest is the inscription of Sir James and his
wife, Barbara, who, when she died in 1639, was 'much
comforted by the sight of 193 of his children and their
offspring at the age of 86 years'. She had 14 children.
The couple were buried at **Calthorpe,** a tiny church
with no windows on the north side. Two admirals, Sir
John Narborough and Sir Cloudesley Shovell, were
christened there in the 17th century.

CAVELL, Edith (1865-1915), nurse and patriot. Matron
at Brussels Nurses' Training Institute, which was a Red
Cross centre in the Great War. She acted as an agent
for the Allies, helping Allied fugitives to escape. She
was shot by the Germans, notwithstanding the efforts
of the American and Spanish Ambassadors in Brussels,
and wide condemnation.
Her body was brought to England and interred in
Norwich Cathedral, later moved to St Martin's, Palace
Plain. She has a statue in Tombland outside the Maid's
Head Hotel, one of the claimants for the title of the
country's oldest inn. There is a memorial window in the
church at **Swardeston,** her birthplace, and part of a
wooden cross from her first grave. A portrait in
Swardeston village room, which she and her sister
helped to build. Their father was vicar for 46 years.
*Her statue outside the National Portrait Gallery,
London, bears her words: 'Patriotism is not enough. I
must have no hatred or bitterness for anyone.'*

*CHAPMAN, John (15th century), traditionally a
Swaffham pedlar. Legend has it that he dreamed of
hearing good news on London Bridge. There a shop-
keeper, who did not know him, mocked him, saying
unexpectedly that he himself had dreamed of a treasure
under a pear tree in the garden of a John Chapman of
Swaffham. The pedlar went back and did find a money
hoard. In gratitude he built the north aisle of **Swaffham**
church, where a pew is carved with the figure of a
pedlar (or chapman). Some say that Chapman was a
wealthy merchant. A wooden sign depicts the Pedlar of
Swaffham.
In the south transept of the 15th century church

(splendid double hammerbeam roof) is a monument to Catherine Steward, grandmother of Oliver Cromwell. Swaffham has a domed market cross. There is a reconstruction of a prehistoric settlement, Iceni Village, and museum at nearby Cockley Cley.

COKE, Sir Edward (1552–1634), lawyer. Black and white marble tomb at **Tittleshall-cum-Godwick;** a black and white career. As Attorney General he made a vindictive, abusive prosecutor of Essex, Raleigh and others. Then he changed to defending the law against the crown and, despite the enmity of Francis Bacon, who had him dismissed from office, championing the House of Commons. He had earlier bought Godwick and Holkham, but retired to Stoke Poges, where he consolidated his reputation as one of the greatest lawyers by massive compilations and commentaries.
Buried, as he wished, beside his first wife, Bridget Paston, and eight children in St Mary's Church. Nicholas Stone was paid £400 for Coke's monument, which shows him recumbent.

COKE, Thomas William, 1st earl of Leicester (second creation) (1754–1842), 'Coke of Norfolk', agricultural innovator. A Whig, at 22 he inherited a great fortune, plus Holkham Hall, but as the Whigs were not in office, he turned to farming, with almost unbelievable success. His annual rent-roll increased ten-fold as he improved soil, crops and livestock. He gave long leases to satisfactory tenants, thus providing work locally as well as food nationally. He anticipated agricultural shows with the 'Holkham Shearings' for up to 700 British and foreign farming enthusiasts, who were entertained lavishly. When George III told Coke that he had enough land and mustn't buy any more, Coke asked for one further acre and, permission granted, acquired it – but it was Castle Acre, an estate comprising 3,000 acres!
Roubiliac made Coke's bust and that of his Countess in **Tittleshall** church. North of Holkham Hall is a monument from the tenants. Also in the church is a large marble relief by Nollekens, showing Mrs Coke (died 1800), leaning on a broken column, an angel on clouds above holding out his hand to her.

COWPER, William (1731-1800), poet. Suffered from mental depression, improved at Olney, Huntingdonshire, with Mrs Mary Unwin as a devoted companion, but worsened through the influence of Calvinist ex-slaver parson, John Newton (who wrote 'Amazing Grace'): under pressure from Newton, Cowper believed he was literally damned. Cowper wrote 'God moves in a mysterious way', later the very different comic 'John Gilpin', later still 'The loss of the *Royal George*' and much else, including a translation of Homer, criticised as being too Miltonic. His letters are delightful. He coined the epigram 'God made the country, and man made the town'. Mental troubles continued to plague him. A very gentle man, he was a keen gardener, raising vegetables under glass - his cucumbers were celebrated. He kept small birds and three pet hares.
Died **East Dereham,** and buried in St Thomas's Chapel. Memorial by Flaxman. Window above shows Cowper with dog and pet hares. The Congregational chapel is on the site of the house where he died, a memorial inscription quoting from his long poem *The Task*.

CRANE, Sir Francis (died c.1636), courtier. Very wealthy, very lucky - he got £2,000 in 1619 from James I to support a tapestry enterprise in a house Crane built in High Street, Mortlake, and was made director. The King granted £1,000 a year and brought over skilled Flemish artisans. Crane also received money for the tapestry concern from the sale of honours. Other courtiers envious, accusing him of excessive profits, perhaps rightly. To Paris for health reasons and died there.
Buried **Wood Rising,** where he urged his wife to live. Crane's arms on brass in ledger stone. Also the tomb of Sir Richard Southwell (1564), 'one of the most unpleasant and unscrupulous of Tudor self-seekers' (Mee).
Deserted villages have been discovered around Wood Rising.

CROME, John ('Old') (1768-1821), landscape painter. 'Old' to distinguish him from his painter son 'Young' John Barney Crome. Son of a weaver. His famous

paintings were done by Old Crome on Sundays and holi-
days, for he supported a large family as full-time
drawing master. At 12 errand boy to Dr Edward Rigby
of Norwich, who helped Crome's seven-year apprentice-
ship to a sign-painter, learning to grind and apply
colours. He worked for the same master as a journey-
man, but began to do work on his own. Crome was
always poor, even though he had patrons. Helped found
the Norwich Society of Arts, 1803. A successful and
influential teacher, but had no reputation as a painter
in his lifetime, rarely getting fifty shillings for a
canvas. Early practised out-of-doors painting, unusual in
his day. His etchings are now highly regarded.
Buried in the 15th century St George's-in-Colegate,
Norwich; the church's early 19th century fittings well
restored since World War II.

DESPENSER, Henry le (1341-1406), bishop of Norwich.
Known as the warlike bishop, he led the charge
'grinding his teeth... like a wild boar' at the defeat of
the peasants under John (or Geoffrey) Litester, dyer, of
Felmingham, seeking to abolish serfdom, near North
Walsham, 1381. The next year led Pope Urban VI's
forces on a Crusade against anti-Pope Clement VII, but
defeated in Flanders. A ferocious opponent of the
Lollards, for John Wyclif denounced the bishop's
crusade. Despenser supported Richard II and was imprisoned for it, but subsequently released. Became
Bishop of Norwich in 1370.
Buried before the high altar, **Norwich** Cathedral. The
Despenser retable, showing the crucified Christ, in St
Luke's Chapel the 'most magnificent piece of 14th
century painting in East Anglia' (Mee), found 1847 face
down as a table-top, carefully restored 1958.

DULEEP SINGH, Prince Frederick. (1868-1926). Son of
Maharajah Duleep Singh. Prince Frederick served with
the Suffolk Yeomanry, the the Norfolk Yeomanry (in
France 1917-19). He lived as an East Anglian gentleman
and wrote archaeological articles on Suffolk and
Norfolk, also contributing to the *Burlington Magazine.*
In 1910 he pleaded in *Country Life* for the preservation

of the picturesque 17th century bridge, condemned as unsafe, of four irregular arches over the Little Ouse at Brandon. A new bridge was erected only in 1952-3.
The Prince had an estate at **Blo Norton,** where he was buried.

EDWARDS, Sir George (1850-1933), pioneer of farm-workers' trade union. The son of a Marsham labourer. Too poor to have any schooling, his wife devotedly taught him to read. A strong religious bent, being a local preacher for the Primitive Methodists. He took up the cause of agricultural workers and, despite prolonged opposition, founded the National Union of Land Workers. MP 1923-4. Knighted 1930.
Buried **Fakenham;** memorial in the cemetery.
Church has a fine tower and a carved screen.

ELWIN, Rev. Whitwell (1815-1900), parson, architect and editor. Rector of Booton 1849, built himself a rectory, built village school, rebuilt church ('the cathedral of the Fields') at his own cost. 'Perhaps the most enthralling ecclesiastical curiosity in Norfolk', the church has been called. "Very naughty, but built in the right spirit," Sir Edwin Lutyens commented. Elwin edited John Murray's *Quarterly Review* from Booton. His friends included Scott, Thackeray, and Lockhart. Elwin's correspondence with Lady Emily Lutyens, *A Blessed Girl,* published 1953. Elwin left his property at Booton to the Lutyens family.
Buried **Booton** churchyard.
The church which excited comment has thickets of exterior pinnacles. The hammerbeam roof has been criticised as too massive and the angels lean out so far that they recall the figure-heads of boats, their maker's real occupation, one critic said somewhat waspishly.

ERPINGHAM. Sir Thomas (1357-1428), soldier. The 'good white head' of this 'most kind gentleman' known from Shakespeare's *Henry V,* when the king borrows his cloak. Erpingham supported John of Gaunt and landed at Ravenspur in 1399 with Bolingbroke (Henry IV). His loyalty was richly rewarded. He commanded the archers at Agincourt, 1415. Lived at Blickling and then Norwich, where he built the splendid Erpingham Gate facing the Cathedral.

Often thought to be buried in **Norwich** Cathedral, where he has a memorial window, but now said to be buried at **Erpingham.** He built the south aisle of the church there and the west tower with the family name round the parapet. His father, Sir John, buried there, 1370. Military brass (to Sir Thomas?), 1416.

FASTOLF, Sir John (c.1378-1459), landholder and soldier. Quite unlike Shakespeare's Falstaff: brave, but bad-tempered, quarrelsome, unforgiving, grasping and certainly not fond of jests. At Agincourt, but defeated by Joan of Arc. He was governor of the Bastille and, as ambassador, negotiated the peace settlement. Acquired various estates, having John Paston as his legal adviser. Built himself Caister Castle of local brick in Rhenish moated style, the only English example (turned into a motor museum). Funded building of the philosophy schools at Cambridge and eventually endowment of Magdalene College, Oxford.

Buried St Benet's Abbey, south of **Ludham.** An open-air service each first Sunday in August is conducted by the Bishop of Norwich to commemorate the appointment of the abbot to the see at the Dissolution, both titles subsequently held by the Bishop.

Ludham church dedicated to St Catherine, whose wheel appears in decoration of the roof; on the screen St Apollinaria with a tooth - she was the patron saint of toothache-sufferers.

FISHER, John Arbuthnot, 1st baron Fisher of Kilverstone (1841-1920), admiral and administrator. A passionate advocate of a strong British navy, associated with the huge shipbuilding programme of 1889, also with the Dreadnought programme. He initiated reforms for training and modernisation and increased efficiency. A formidable personality that suffuses his own account of his career, beginning as a cadet in the Crimean War, followed by much service afloat - torpedo, gunnery, ordnance - and ashore; high office (3rd Sea Lord and

Controller of the Navy) and stormy episodes. He resigned 1910 and was recalled 1914; resigned again over the Dardanelles.

A public naval funeral at Westminster Abbey, then interment at remote **Kilverstone,** a small church down a track from the village green.

GURNEY, Anna (1795-1857), scholar and translator. A remarkable member of a remarkable family. Though paralysed as an infant, Anna led a full, even happy life. Her translation of the *Anglo-Saxon Chronicle* appeared 1819. Lived at Northrepps Cottage, near Cromer. Bought a life-saving apparatus (see Manby) and, on occasion, was carried down to the beach to direct its use. The first woman member of the British Archaeological Association.

Buried **Overstrand.**

The restored church there has a pulpit given by Lady Florence Barclay, author of The Rosary, 1909. Lady Battersea, the fashionable Liberal hostess before the Great War, gave Italian ironwork for the lamps in the chancel.

HAGGARD, Sir Henry Rider (1856-1925), novelist and agricultural expert. As a young man Haggard held official posts in South Africa, 1875-9, and turned his first-hand knowledge of Africa to account in *King Solomon's Mines,* 1885, which brought him immediate fame, increased by *She,* 1887. His story-telling, imaginative use of exotic settings (not only African) and his vigorously sketched characters helped maintain his popularity with readers of some 30 tales. Married a Norfolk heiress in 1880, settling in Ditchingham 1889. He made himself an authority on Empire migration, agricultural matters at home and overseas (*Rural England,* 1902, is one of his best works) and social conditions, with an interest in the Salvation Army. Knighted 1912. Biography by D S Higgins, 1981.

Haggard was cremated, his ashes being buried under a black marble slab in 15th century **Ditchingham** church, built on a bank among trees away from the village.

Serpentine lake in park attributed to Capability Brown.

HARBORNE, William (died 1617), first English ambassador to Turkey. Elizabeth I's choice for the post, in which Harborne was very successful. He secured the release of many English captives and made navigation in Turkish waters much safer for English ships. This led to increased opportunities for trade, which Harborne worked hard to stimulate. He had an uncomfortable and dangerous return journey, described in Hakluyt's *Voyages*, bringing with him a letter from the sultan for the queen, couched in excessively flowery language.
Buried in remote **Mundham.**
The church has a richly carved Norman doorway in the south porch, a simpler Norman doorway in the north porch, and a 15th century screen with an old hourglass bracket.

HARE, Sarah (died 1744), a warning against profaning the Sabbath. She was guilty - she sewed on a Sunday, pricked her finger and died of blood poisoning. She directed the making of her effigy in wax to be displayed inside a (locked) mahogany cabinet in the brick Hare Chapel, **Stow Bardolph** church. Also in the Chapel, Sir Thomas Hare (died 1693), in Roman armour, but full bottomed wig; Sarah's sister, Susannah (they were his daughters), by Scheemakers, 1741.
It was Nicholas Hare who built Stow Bardolph Hall in 1589 for £40,000. Much later Field Marshal Lord Roberts placed a brass in the church in memory of James William Adams, rector 1895-1902, the first chaplain to receive the Victoria Cross.

HIGDON, Tom (died 1939) and Kitty (died 1943), teachers. Involved in the longest British strike, from 1914 to 1939, started by 66 out of 72 schoolchildren. The Higdons, Christian Socialists, came to Burston in south Norfolk in 1911. Tom recruited farm labourers into a trade union and on to the village council, displeasing local farmers. The rector was offended by Kitty's independent attitude as schoolmistress and worked with farmers to dismiss her, first on the grounds of brutality (a failed frame-up), at last successfully for 'disrespect'. Pupil Violet Potter led a walk-out. Teaching continued on the village green, then

Blickling Hall

in a carpenter's shop. A new school built on the green in 1917 with contributions from sympathisers; pupils also came from outside the village.
Higdons buried in **Burston** churchyard.

HOBART, John, 2nd earl of Buckinghamshire (1723-93), politician. Ambassador to Catherine the Great's Russia, 1762-5; Lord Lieutenant of Ireland, 1776-80, where he was quite unable to cope with the difficulties. Horace Walpole called him 'Clearcake: fat, fair, sweet and seen through in a moment'.
Buried **Blickling** (pyramid tomb in park).
Jacobean Hall one of the finest in England. Sir Thomas Erpingham lived in previous Hall, then Sir John Fastolf, who sold it to Ann Boleyn's grandfather. Ann lived there as a child. Brasses in the church to Boleyn ladies, but not Ann. The present Hall built by Sir Henry Hobart, Lord Chief Justice.

*HUME, Joseph (1777-1865), radical. A surgeon with the East India Company, retiring wealthy at 30. For thirty years leader of Radical party in Parliament, adding 'retrenchment' to the party's slogan (Peace and Reform). Through him the Sinking Fund was abandoned, and the Combination Laws repealed. He helped the abolition of flogging in the army, press-ganging and the contemporary system of imprisonment for debt. He lived at Somerton House, Winterton, renamed Burnley Hall after his wife's maiden name.
Hume is buried at Kensal Green, London, but there is a tablet in **Winterton** church, its flint and stone tower visible for miles inland and far out to sea.
Nearby nature reserve of about 250 acres.

JENKINS, John (1592-1678), composer. His output included a great deal of chamber music, which could be played by amateurs, no doubt because he lived with patrons much of his life. Residential post with the Le Strange family of Hunstanton, next with Norths, then with Wodehouses at Kimberley.
Memorial and epitaph in **Kimberley** church (much restored), near park gates and picturesque village green.
Capability Brown worked on the park, 1762.

*JULIAN, Mother (Juliana) (1342?-1430), anchoress. She, servant and cat lived in a cell attached to St Julian's Church, Norwich. Perhaps educated at nearby Carrow Abbey. Penguin Classic of her *Revelations of Divine Love*, meditations on her visions. Gave advice and help to many, including Margery Kempe. The church nearly destroyed by bombs in 1942, but rebuilt. Mother Julian's cell as side chapel.
There is a stained glass window to her (with cat) in **Norwich** Cathedral.

*KEMPE (nee Brunham), Margery (c.1373-after 1436), mystic. Fervently devout, very objectionable through uncontrolled fits of weeping and bumptious habits, such as her obstinate refusal to eat meat. Born in King's Lynn, father a merchant who was several times mayor. Her husband John Kempe of Lynn to whom she bore many children. A pilgrim (unpopular with the others) to Jerusalem and Rome, 1414-15; to St James of Compostella later. Went to Dantzig about 1433 with her widowed daughter-in-law, returning all the way alone. Around 1436 she dictated the *Book of Margery Kemp* the first autobiography in English; it was only discovered in 1936 in a Lancashire library.
Presumably buried **King's Lynn.** Which church? St Margaret's has perhaps the best claim, for in 1421 the intervention of Margery Kempe is said to have saved it from fire. It has two western towers and two of the most important brasses in England. Another strong claimant is the huge church of St Nicholas, founded 1146, but not built for about 300 years. Here, during the annual King's Lynn Festival, distinguished orchestral concerts are given, sometimes attended by royalty.
King's Lynn is a treasury of fine buildings, outstanding being the Guildhall of the Holy Trinity (1423) and its modern counterpart, the Town Hall, holding King John's Sword and his Cup (not really John's, but magnificent) among the regalia. Then there is the 15th century St George's Guildhall, transformed into a theatre where Shakespeare may have acted, later turned into a warehouse and now a theatre again, prominent in the Lynn Festival. The Custom House, rightly admired, was

designed by Henry Bell, twice Mayor of King's Lynn, and architect also of the Duke's Head Hotel (1689) and Clifton House.

*KERR, Philip Henry, 11th marquis of Lothian (1882-1940), statesman and journalist. One of Lord Milner's 'young men'. A founder of *Round Table* magazine in 1910, to promote the unity of British Commonwealth. Private secretary to Lloyd George 1916-21. Secretary to the Rhodes trustees, 1925. Ambassador to the United States, 1939, working to improve American understanding of Britain. He left the Blickling estate to the National Trust.
Died America, ashes in National Cemetery, Arlington, later removed to Jedburgh. Memorial in **Blickling** parish church (also one to 8th marquis by G F Watts).

LE STRANGE, Hamon (1840-1918), developer of Hunstanton. The coming of the railway in 1862 inspired him to develop New Hunstanton as a pleasure resort. The architect Butterfield was called in to design St Edward's church. After recovery from typhoid, the Prince of Wales (later Edward VII) came to Hunstanton for convalescence and his stay added to the new resort's reputation.
Le Strange buried in **Old Hunstanton** church, where the long-established family has several monuments, including a tomb chest to Henry (1485) and a brass to Sir Roger (1506).
The head of the family bears the title Hereditary Lord High Admiral of the Wash. Son of an earlier Sir Hamon was Sir Roger L'Estrange (1616-1704), who had an exciting life in Tory political adventures, started early newspapers, wrote many books and pamphlets and made first English translation of Aesop's Fables, 1692. John Jenkins was family musician to the Le Stranges.
P G Wodehouse stayed at Hunstanton Hall in the 1920s and used it as the setting for his Money for Nothing.

*LINCOLN, Samuel (born 1622), weaver, ancestor of Abraham Lincoln. Emigrated 1638 to North America. Baptised at Hingham, which has many American associations. Robert Peck, rector, left for Massachusetts in 1620 with 21 families and founded new town of

Hingham. Close links maintained between the two
Hinghams. Bust of Abraham Lincoln presented by sub-
scription to Norfolk **Hingham** in 1919.
*The church has a small knob turret above the tower
stair. The east window has 15th century continental
glass. Among other features are the only bushel
measure in a church; and a monument to Thomas, Lord
Morley (died 1435), Marshal of Ireland, descendant of
Sir Robert de Morley, Admiral of the Fleet at Sluys,
1340, when the French had to cede control of the
Channel.*

LOSINGA, Herbert (1054?-1119), first bishop of
Norwich and founder of the Cathedral. He was made
abbot of Ramsay in 1087 by William Rufus. He founded
St Nicholas's Church, Great Yarmouth and St
Margaret's at Lynn, giving the town the name of Lynn
Episcopi, changed by Henry VIII to Lynn Regis at the
Dissolution. Losinga had the Pope's approval to move his
see from Thetford to Norwich. He was high in the
favour of Henry I and Queen Matilda. In Norwich
Cathedral his St Saviour's Chapel was replaced in 1250
by a Lady Chapel; a new St Saviour's Chapel was built
in the 1930s at a Great War memorial and is the
regimental chapel of the Royal Norfolks.
Near the bishop's throne in **Norwich** Cathedral is an
effigy usually accepted as Losinga's.
*Magnificent Cathedral begun 1096, completed by middle
of the 12th century; rebuilding later. Extremely long
nave, the massive pillars of the arcades, its arches and
shafts repeated in the gallery; height and austerity of
the chancel emphasised by clerestory and rib vault.*

MANBY, Captain George William (1765-1854), inventor.
Born Denver. A fellow pupil of Horatio Nelson at
Downham Market. Still a boy, Manby fired a rope by
rocket over Downham church. Later, as the barracks
master at Yarmouth in 1807, he was forced to watch
helpless as men drowned in a shipwreck, he remembered
his youthful feat and devised a mortar to fire a rocket
with line attached, practising from the stumpy brick
tower of Hilgay church. His apparatus proved its worth

within a year and was widely adopted; said to have saved more sailors than died in battle. Manby made improvements in the construction of lifeboats too and devised a fire-extinguisher containing liquid under pressure.

He died at Yarmouth, but was buried next to his parents at **Hilgay,** where his father, lord of the manor, lived in the Elizabethan brick-built Wood Hall.

MARRYAT, Captain Frederick (1792-1848), sailor and novelist. Into the navy at 14, he saw much action and had many adventures, some under Lord Cochrane. He gave up the sea in 1830 and drew on his experiences in such books as *Peter Simple,* 1831, *Mr Midshipman Easy,* 1836 and *Masterman Ready,* 1841. In North America, 1837-8. For some years he owned Langham manor, going there in 1843 to run the farm, but couldn't make a profit. He made money while there by writing *Children of the New Forest* and other books. It is said that once, when staying at Raynham Hall (the Townshend house), Marryat saw the velvet-clad figure of the local ghost, the Brown Lady, with empty eye-sockets, and fired his pistol at her, the bullets passing through the shade and lodging in the door.

Marryat buried at **Langham** churchyard, appropriately near the salt marshes.

The church has Burne-Jones glass in the northeast nave window. The village pub has been given custody of the Union Jack flown by Cindy Buxton and Annie Price, naturalists and film-makers, on South Georgia during the Argentine occupation.

MARTIN, Sarah (1791-1845), pioneer of prison reform. A humble dressmaker, she turned to religion when 19 and, despite her lack of resources, felt she must aid women prisoners. After years of obstruction, she was at last allowed to visit Yarmouth Tollhouse, where she taught religion, reading and writing. Soon she added needlework, sold the things they made and used the money for the women's good. She helped find employment for some of the men and looked after the children. She helped workhouse inmates too and gave two nights a week to school for factory girls. The

Inspector of Prisons in reports, 1835-44, testified to the success of her work. In 1841 she was persuaded to accept payment of £12 a year, but her health was already broken.

Buried **Caister** churchyard.

Modern resort of Caister is built on the site of a Roman walled town, much studied, some preserved for visitors. Saxons settled in the ruins after the Roman withdrawal, but the Danes chose the site that became the centre of modern Caister.

Also in Caister churchyard (and memorial window in church) a monument to nine Caister lifeboatmen who perished in 1901.

There is a memorial window to Sarah Martin in **Yarmouth** parish church; subscribers included Bishop Stanley, who said "I would canonise Sarah Martin if I could."

MONCK, [Walter] Nugent [Bligh] (1878-1958), founder of the Maddermarket Theatre, Norwich (madder being a root yielding a red dye). Monck founded the Norwich Players in 1911 and he produced more than 300 plays for them, including all Shakespeare. In 1926 he took over the Maddermarket building which had been a Roman Catholic church, a Salvation Army hall and a factory and made of it an Elizabethan-type theatre. Monck's productions were entertaining, but also of cultural and educational merit. Associated with his work for the theatre were the pageants that Monck staged, among them Norwich 1926 and Ipswich 1930.

Monck was cremated and his ashes interred at St John Maddermarket, **Norwich.**

MOTTEUX, John, 19th century lord of the manor, Beachamwell. Motteux was injured in a cab accident in Piccadilly, involving Charles Spencer Cowper, stepson of Lord Palmerston. Cowper was very solicitous and insisted on caring for Motteux, starting a long friendship. In gratitude Motteux bequeathed to Cowper his Norfolk estates, which included Sandringham, later sold to the Prince of Wales (Edward VII). Cowper put up a tablet to Motteux's memory in **Beachamwell** church.

This is the only surviving one of three churches

formerly existing at Beachamwell. It is St Mary's, partly thatched, with a round tower and octagonal belfry. The remains of a second church are to the south of the village and the ruins (much damaged tower and walls) of a third near the hall in the park. West of the village is the ancient earthwork of the Devil's Dyke.

MOTTRAM, R[alph] H[ale] (1883-1971), novelist, banker and magistrate. Famous for his *Spanish Farm* trilogy of novels, for which he was awarded the Hawthornden Prize; they describe the life of British troops in Flanders during the Great War and the war's effect on the farm. A friend of John Galsworthy, whose influence has been traced in Mottram's writing, from 1904 until Galsworthy's death in 1933. Mottram wrote a biography of Galsworthy and his wife. Although Mottram began in banking and continued there for many years, he wrote many other novels, *A History of Financial Speculation*, 1929, and *History of the East India Company*, 1940. Before 1914, as J Marjoram, he published two volumes of verse. His autobiography is entitled *Window Seat, or Life Observed*, 1954.
Buried Rosary Cemetery, **Norwich**, as is Jeremiah Colman (1830-98), of the great mustard firm. Russell James Colman (1860-1946), died Norwich, was cremated and commemorated by a service in St Peter Mancroft.

NELSON, Rev. Edmund (1722-1802), father of Horatio Nelson (1758-1805), rector of **Burnham Thorpe** (1755-1802), buried there with other members of the family (Lord Nelson, of course, in St Paul's, London).
The church has the font in which Horatio was baptised and many other momentoes of the Admiral. His bust over his father's grave was given by the London Society of East Anglians at the centenary of Trafalgar. The new altar, 1911, dedicated to Lord Nelson and those whose perished with him. Timbers of the Victory used for the cross under the chancel arch and for the lectern, given by the Lords of the Admiralty in 1877. Other naval momentoes: two white ensigns from HMS Nelson after being taken out of service at the end of

World War II; flags from HMS Indomitable at the Battle of Jutland, 1916. The village hall is a memorial to Lord Nelson, who took as his title Baron Nelson of the Nile and Burnham Thorpe.

*PAINE, Thomas (Tom) (1737-1809), revolutionary writer. Active in the American and the French Revolutions. Benjamin Franklin persuaded Paine to go to America, where he advocated independence, was made secretary to the Committee of Foreign Affairs, and helped frame the Constitution. Back in England in time for the French Revolution. The wide sales and wider influence of his *The Rights of Man* alarmed men of property. Threatened, Paine fled to France, where he was elected member of the Convention. Imprisoned, however, for trying to save the King's life. He wrote *The Age of Reason* in prison. When released he returned to America, but his revolutionary past and the 'atheism' of *The Age of Reason'* told against him. He died in obscurity, his reputation reviving this century.

Tom Paine's bones are lost. A statue given by the Thomas Paine Society of America has been erected (to raised eyebrows!) in **Thetford,** his birthplace, outside the offices of the Borough Council, which used to be James I's hunting lodge.

Thetford has the great mound of a Norman castle, the 14th century gateway, three storeys high, of the Cluniac Priory of Our Lady, founded in the 12th century, and one of the oldest boys' schools in England, founded 1566.

PASTON family. Famous for their exchange of about a thousand letters in English vividly revealing what it was like to live before, during and after the Wars of the Roses: personal details, household affairs, marriages, business matters, lawsuits, affrays, national and international events.

Sir William Paston, justice of the Common Bench, 'the Good Judge' (1378-1444). Able and hard-working, he established the family fortune. Buried in the Chapel of Our Lady, **Norwich** Cathedral.

John I (1421-66), legal adviser to Sir John Fastolf,

claimed his estates, but the Pastons had to struggle for them against the Dukes of Norfolk and Suffolk. John Paston married Margaret Mautby, who wrote some of the best letters. In 1449 she was driven out of Gresham (bought from Geoffrey Chaucer's son Thomas) by Lord Moleyns with a force of about 1,000 men and the fortified manor was destroyed. In 1465 John de la Pole, 2nd duke of Suffolk, destroyed Hellesdon (east of Norwich), another of the Paston manors. John was buried in **Bromholm** Priory, near Bacton, his mourners almost suffocated by the 'reke of the torches of the dirge'.

The Priory, famous after claiming to have a piece of the True Cross, was mentioned by the Miller's Wife in Chaucer's Canterbury Tales and by Piers Plowman, both of whom call on Bromholm Cross for aid.

John's wife, Margaret, was buried in 1484 in **Mautby** thatched church, her tomb disappearing in the 18th century when part of the church was ruined.

Bacton was 'one of the prettiest places in Norfolk' when Pevsner visited it, but since then North Sea gas has been brought ashore at the Bacton terminal.

Sir Clement (1515?-98), courtier. Wounded and left for dead at the Battle of Pinkie, 1547. Sheriff of Norfolk, 1588. High in fame under Henry VII, Protector Somerset, Mary and Elizabeth. Built Oxnead Hall by the River Bure, grandest of the Paston houses; only one wing remains. Ironically, fountains and statues from Oxnead went to the Paston's rivals, the Hobarts, at Blickling.

Alabaster effigy of Sir Clement on a tomb chest in the little church of **Oxnead.** Also a striking bust of Lady Katherine Paston (nee Knevel) (1629), for which Nicholas Stone was 'very extraordinarily entertained, and pay'd for it £340'.

Church has 17th and 18th century additions in tower, porches and east gable.

Sir William IV (1479?-1554), lawyer and courtier. Buried **Paston**, like others of the family.

Church with thatched roof; some 14th century paintings uncovered 1922, including a huge St Christopher.

Sir William (died 1610). Founded North Walsham

Grammar School, 1606. Many distinguished pupils. While Nelson was there he stole pears from the headmaster's garden to share with the other boys, none of whom dared to go. Sir William also endowed Gonville & Caius College, Cambridge.

He designed his own tomb in **North Walsham** church, an armoured alabaster figure with wall monument and a display of Paston arms and shields of their marriage connections; he paid £200 for having the tomb made.

North Walsham market cross in market place.

The only surviving Paston house, at Barmingham Winter, was built in 1612.

It passed to the Mott family in 1775; Humphrey Repton altered the interior and the south front in 1805.

The Pastons flourished under the Stuarts, Sir Robert becoming Earl of Yarmouth. His son, however, wasted the estates, which were sold to Lord Anson for some of the prize money from his voyage round the world. Title extinct, 1732.

POCAHONTAS see John ROLFE.

PRATT, Sir Roger (1620-85), architect. Important, if sometimes overlooked, for the influence of his ideas and practice. He studied buildings during a long tour of the continent 1643-9, but had no formal training. On his return was invited by a relative to supervise the building of Italianate Coleshill House, Berkshire. Inigo Jones and John Webb also involved. Pratt built only five houses, the sole remaining one - a beauty - is Kingston Lacy, Dorset. Appointed with Wren and May to supervise the rebuilding of London after the Great Fire. Knighted 1668 for services.

Buried **Ryston,** where the family associations go back to the 16th century. Pratt re-roofed the church, since considerably restored. Effigy to his wife, 1706, by her second husband.

REPTON, Humphrey (1752-1818), landscape gardener. Third time lucky; he twice failed in business, then prompted by his hobby, botany, turned gardener in 1685. He began as a disciple of Capability Brown and defended him against criticism by Payne Knight and Uvedale Price. Later reacted against Brown's formal approach and developed his own 'picturesque' style, more natural and varied. Enormous and lasting success in 'improving' estates throughout England (and some in Scotland and Ireland). He laid out Russell Square and altered Kensington Gardens in London. He prepared careful studies for clearance and planting in a series of 'red books', many of which survive. They comprise water-colour sketches 'before' and, superimposed on cutout flaps, 'after'. He wrote books on gardening, on local history and on art. He had to retire in 1811 after his spine was injured in an accident while returning with his daughter from a ball. He lived for his last 45 years in Repton Cottage, Hare Street, Romford, Essex, which he had, of course, 'improved'.

Buried at St Michael's, **Aylsham,** a huge church with a damaged tower. Repton's epitaph was re-cut by the Aylsham Society, which planted new roses bushes above his grave.

RIGBY, Dr Edward (1747-1821), surgeon. An estimable man: the Norwich doctor who employed Old Crome as an errand boy. Rigby was present at the Storming of the Bastille, 1789, his 'extreme gladness' turning to 'amazement mingled with alarm' as bloody heads on pikes were carried past. Mayor of Norwich, 1805, where he practised for 53 years. He wrote on scientific and medical subjects. An enthusiast for vaccination; interested in improving agriculture, experimenting on his own farm. At Framlingham Earl he planted many trees.

Buried **Framlingham Earl** in a table tomb, near the Saxon chancel of the small church, with appropriate epitaph: 'A monument to Rigby do you seek?/ On every side the whispering woodlands speak.'

*ROLFE, John (1585-1622), husband of the American Indian Princess Pocahontas (1595?-1617), daughter of Powhattan and legendary saviour of Captain John Smith. Rolfe left Heacham, the family home, for America as a young man, was shipwrecked off the Bermudas, settled in Virginia and introduced tobacco as a crop. John Smith had returned to England after falling ill and

Pocahontas, now converted to Christianity and christened Rebecca, believing him dead, married Rolfe in 1613. He brought her and their infant son Thomas to England, 1616, and she was taken up at Court. She met John Smith again. Said to have lived at Heacham for a time. Pocahontas pined for America and was waiting for a ship when she died of smallpox at Gravesend. Rolfe returned alone to Virginia, though Thomas followed in due course.

Alabaster portrait of Pocahontas at **Heacham** by Ottilia Wallace, who studied with Rodin.

Heacham's tall spire a landmark. Lavender is harvested in high summer at Caley Mill, the largest producer of lavender in the country.

*SAYERS, Dorothy L[eigh] (1893-1957). The enormous church of St Peter at **Upwell**, near Wisbech, has been claimed as the model for 'Fenchurch St Paul' in *The Nine Tailors* a claim inspired no doubt by St Peter's north gallery. Her father was rector of Christchurch, in Upwell parish, but in Cambridgeshire.

A four-sided brass in the church to Sinulphus Bell, 1618, and Mrs Bell 'who never delayed by deeds and good usage to give him content.' Many excellent 18th century headstones in the churchyard.

A steam train used to run from Upwell along the Nene towards Wisbech, passing through English fenland with a Dutch look that would surely have appealed to Hobbema.

*SEAGO, Edward (1910-74), artist. Born Norwich. Very ill as a child, so painted scenes from his bedroom window, but not encouraged by his parents. Largely self-taught. He joined Bevin's Travelling Show when 18 and toured with circuses in Britain and on the continent, writing of his experiences in two books, which he illustrated. He did illustrations for John Masefield. Saw service with the Royal Engineers, 1939-45, serving and painting in Italy with Field Marshal Lord Alexander. He is said to have been involved in espionage. His war pictures exhibited in Norwich and Bristol and he wrote of his war experiences. His autobiography was entitled *A Canvas to Cover*, 1947. He

worked in Ipswich and painted pictures on the Duke of
Edinburgh's world tour. Fond of travel, he liked to sail
his boat across the Channel to Le Havre, then up the
Seine to Paris, painting on the voyage. Lived for some
years at **Ludham,** which has the only surviving trading
whern.
Seago was cremated and his ashes scattered on the
Norfolk marshes.

SEWELL, Anna (1820-78), author of *Black Beauty,* probably the most famous story about a horse, told as
autobiography. Anna, born in Yarmouth, was lame from
childhood and a lifelong invalid, house-bound in her last
years. Her mother Mary (née Wright) (1797-1884)
turned, late in life, to writing, producing improving
books in verse and prose for children. About 1871, at
Old Catton, just outside Norwich, Anna too began to
write, working on *Black Beauty* whenever her health
allowed. Appearing in 1877, it was very successful, with
French, Italian and German translations; the Royal
Society for the Prevention of Cruelty to Animals heart-
ily approved of its denunciation of the bearing-rein and
its avowed aim of increasing sympathetic kindness to
horses.
Father, mother and daughter buried in the Friends'
Burial Ground, **Lamas,** recently sadly neglected.

SKELTON, John (c.1460-1529), poet and satirist. Led a
wild life, marked by buffoonery and practical jokes,
although a priest. He held the benefit of Diss from
1504, though he was mostly in London. His satire
offended Wolsey, but his scholarship was praised by
Caxton and Erasmus. A versatile poet, famous for his
vigorous 'Skeltonic' verse, in short lines of irregular
metre, such as *Phyllyp Sparowe,* a burlesque lament on
a sparrow killed by a cat, and the carryings on of
drunken women at a Leatherhead (Surrey) ale-house,
The Tunning of Elynour Runnyng. Said to have died at
Westminster in sanctuary from Wolsey, but there is a
strong tradition that he came from **Diss** and was buried
there.
The church has a processional passage through the

tower. *Francis Blomefield was familiar with the large mere close by from school days in Diss. There is much of interest nearby, including plants labelled in Braille at Freezen Hall Sanctuary, which is a garden for the blind and for physically or mentally handicapped people. Steam engines are displayed with alpines and perennials at Bressingham Gardens. Banham Zoo and Monkey Sanctuary has interesting cars and motor cycles on view.*

TOWNSHEND, Charles, 2nd viscount (1674-1738), Whig statesman, 'Turnip' Townshend. A long political career, concentrating on foreign affairs, latterly with his brother-in- law, Robert Walpole, who finally ousted him in 1730. Thereafter, at 56, Townshend turned to farming, improving the poor soil on his estate, but even more famous for using Jethro Tull's newly-invented seed-drill for corn and, especially, turnips (hence his nickname). Turnip cultivation cleaned the soil, sheep ate the turnips and manured the land, making possible a corn crop the next year, thus obviating the need for fallow. The practice led to a crop-rotation system.
Townshend buried at **East Raynham** church, with other Townshend monuments including the tall sepulchre for Sir Roger (died 1493), legal adviser to the Pastons; General George, who took over from the dying Wolfe at Quebec; and Sir Charles, the general who had to surrender Kut to the Turks in the Great War.
The church is between a lake and the lovely 17th century Hall, said to be haunted (see Marryat).

WALPOLE, Horace (formally Horatio), 4th earl of Orford (1717-97), author, wit and correspondent - Byron called his letters 'incomparable'. Son (questioned by some) of Sir Robert Walpole, who awarded him state sinecures for life worth about £100,000 a year in our money. A friend of the poet, Thomas Gray. Spent the years 1753-76 converting a coachman's cottage in Twickenham into the battlements, stucco and cloisters of Strawberry Hill,   his 'little Gothic castle with a printing press', as he called it. He wrote *The Castle of Otranto,* 1764, a 'Gothic' romance which has been much imitated. His sprightly, witty letters range over gossip, art, literature, foreign affairs and politics (the Jacobite trials after the '45; the Gordon Riots, etc.). Walpole's *Memoirs of George II and George III were criticised by Macaulay as frivolous, but they make* criticised by Macaulay as frivolous, but they make lively reading, with malicious pen-portraits, like his pillorying of the circumnavigator, Lord Anson, as a man who had gone all round the world, but was never in it and who had a similar physical relationship with his wife. Anson was attacked because he was son-in-law to Philip Yorke (see Cambridgeshire), dubiously accused by Walpole of betraying his father, Sir Robert.

Buried in St James's Church in the park of that great East Anglian house, **Houghton Hall,** built for Sir Robert Walpole, sometimes open to the public; it houses a collection of thousands of model soldiers and other military exhibits.

Cottages formerly round the church were pulled down and re-erected outside Sir Robert's gates.

WALPOLE, Robert, 1st earl of Orford (1676-1745), Whig statesman. He stabilised the Hanoverian succession by ensuring 20 years of prosperity and, thus, satisfaction with the dynasty. In office 1721-42. The 'first Prime Minister' and the first to use No.10 Downing Street officially. Walpole developed cabinet rule - with potential rivals excluded. He established the Sinking Fund to pay off capital and reduce interest on the National Debt. He encouraged trade and industry, keeping taxation low. His foreign policy - peace at any price - was less successful. He lost popularity with the War of Jenkins' Ear against Spain, 1739-48. Irked by *The Beggar's Opera* and other anti-government satires, Walpole reduced the number of theatres by the Licensing Act, 1737, incidentally ending Henry Fielding's career as a busy playwright and turning his mind to writing novels.

Walpole is buried in St Martin's Church, **Houghton Hall.**

*WALSTAN, Saint (c.965-1016). Made Bawburgh a place of pilgrimage. There is a tower called Slipper House

where pilgrims left their shoes. Walstan took a vow of
poverty after a vision and spent his life as a farm-
worker, although his parents were wealthy; his mother
was St Blide, buried at Martham. A shrine to him built,
as he requested, at the stopping place of his funeral
cart drawn by a pair of oxen given him by his master;
destroyed under Henry VIII, Walstan's bones being
burned and scattered. **Bawburgh** church incorporates
some of his chapel walls and its round tower may be
from his time. North of the church is a well where the
oxen are said to have paused.
Old water mill formerly used for paper-making.

WILLIAMSON (née Hobart), Lady Dionis (died 1684).
Remembered for her generous donations for rebuilding
after the Great Fire of London, 1666. She gave £2,000
for re-building St Paul's; £4,000 for St Dunstan-in-the-
East; and £2,000 for St Mary-le-Bow.
Buried Holy Trinity, **Loddon,** a church having a two-
storey south porch with stair turret, in an outstanding
marble sarcophagus, her reclining effigy above it. Other
Hobart family monuments, also the rare subject of the
alleged martydom of little St William of Norwich in
one panel of a screen.
*Jacobean pulpit. Church built by Sir James Hobart,
Attorney General to Henry VII, who also built the
fortifed manor of Hales Hall, recently restored, with
moated gardens and a splendid barn.*

WINDHAM, William III (1750-1810), statesman. A friend
of Burke and Dr Johnson. At first opposed Pitt, but,
alarmed by Jacobins in France and their influence on
English radicals, turned against parliamentary reform.
He remained suspicious of Pitt, though serving for a
time in his ministry. He tried to improve conditions in
the army. He refused a peerage.
Buried in the isolated church in **Felbrigg** park. Bust by
Nollekens on a marble sarcophagus, a monument criticised for obscuring the beautiful sedilia. Grinling Gibbons
was paid £50 for the monument to William Windham I
(1691). There is an outstanding military brass to Sir
Symon de Felbrigg, standard-bearer to Richard II.

The Norfolk historian, R W Ketton-Cremer, left the lovely Jacobean Felbrigg Hall to the National Trust.

WOODFORDE, Rev. James (1740-1803), diarist. For 29 years rector of Weston Longville, nearly 44 years a diarist. His work, begun while at university, published as *The Diary of a Country Parson* in several volumes from 1924. He commented tolerantly on neighbours, parish officials, his congregation and his servants. Fond of his food - innumerable details of his meals - and his drink (rum, bought from smuggler Andrews, who also supplied tea and silk handkerchiefs at prices specified). Woodforde took cures, sometimes very odd, for sundry ailments. Occasionally went to Norwich for the shops, the theatre or a concert. Fond of riding, gardening and angling, while health permitted. A bachelor, his niece, Nancy, kept house for him.

A memorial in the chancel, **Weston Longville** church; portrait by nephew, Samuel Woodforde, RA, in vestry.

The church has a short, square tower, a big pew for the Custance family (died out this century) and a Jesse Tree wall painting discovered in 1937.

*WYTHBURGA, Saint (died 654), sister of Etheldreda (see Cambridgeshire) and of Sexburga and Werburga, also buried Ely. Wythburga founded the nunnery and church at East Dereham, both destroyed by the Danes.

She was buried in **East Dereham** churchyard, where a spring of healing water rose (converted in the 18th century to a public bath), still visible as a well. Her relics were coveted for their miraculous powers by the Abbot of Ely, who, in 987, had the Saint's body stolen after making local people drunk. His raiders were pursued by the Dereham men and nearly caught at Brandon, but there the despoilers took to the water and the pursuers, having no boats, had to content themselves with throwing stones from the .bank.

The present church has a 16th century detached tower with a great clock.

Norwich Cathedral

Suffolk

AIRY, George Biddell (1801-92), Astronomer Royal, 'Father of Greenwich Observatory', where he opened the magnetic and meteorological department in 1838, designing many of the instruments himself. He determined the mean density of the Earth, 1854. He expanded astronomical photography, especially of the sun and sunspots. He was very interested in eclipses. His wide abilities were recognised in connection with the launch of the *Great Eastern*, Brunel's steamship; laying transatlantic cable; chimes of Westminster and smoke abatement. A sufferer from astigmatism, the

DENNINGTON PARISH CHURCH.

Dennington

first to call attention to this defect.
Buried **Playford,** next to Thomas Clarkson.
The church, overlooking the village in the valley, has an outstanding brass effigy to Sir George Felbrigg (1400), whose house was probably on the site of the moated Hall and who built the tower-porch.

ANDERSON (née Garrett), Elizabeth Garrett (1836-1917), England's first woman doctor. The medical profession didn't recognise women at the time, so she was licensed by the Society of Apothecaries, which amended its charter to prevent any other woman from qualifying. She opened Marylebone dispensary for women and children, later a hospital (given her name), the first in Europe staffed by women and where women treated women. Robert Browning, a family friend, supported Dr Anderson's election to the London School Board. Paris awarded her a degree before the British Medical Association accepted her as a member. A lecturer at the London School for Medical Women. For many years president of the East Anglian branch of the B.M.A. The first woman mayor in England - of Aldeburgh.
Buried **Aldeburgh** churchyard beside her parents. Her suffragette sister Millicent married blind Harry Fawcett (see Cambridgeshire).

BARDOLPH, William Philipp, Lord Bardolph (died 1441), Treasurer to Henry V's household. Perhaps the original of Bardolph in Shakespeare's *Henry IV, Part II*. Fought at Harfleur and Agincourt under Henry V.
Wanted a quiet funeral, only 20 torches aflame when his body entered a town or city. Given an alabaster, pinnacled tomb (with wife) in **Dennington** church, called 'intensely exciting' (Shell Guide).
The church's features range from a 17th century double-decker pulpit, 18th century box pews, a hanging pyx with cover, to 15th century bench ends, one carved with a Skiapod, human in shape except that his gigantic webbed feet were used as a sunshade.

BARNARDISTON, Sir Samuel (1620-1707), merchant. The first man to be called 'Roundhead': seeing his unfashionably short hair, Queen Henrietta Maria remarked, "What a handsome young roundhead is there", and the term was then applied to Parliamentarians. Sir Samuel took no part in the Civil War and welcomed Charles II. A governor of the East India Company, very rich from the Levant trade. He was tried by Judge Jeffreys, 1684, after innocent involvement in the Rye House Plot to assassinate Charles II, fined, imprisoned for refusal to pay and released after part payment.

Buried at **Kedington,** among the finest of the Puritan churches. Barnardiston monuments, pews (sex-segregated) made from 15th century screen, and four vaults, one with fireplace, for many Barnardiston coffins, some body-shaped. Sir Samuel donated the Communion rails round the Sanctuary, its altar table on black and white marble floor.

There is a three-decker pulpit with a tester, wig-block at second stage, hourglass in stand on top stage. Single-handed clock on church tower.

BARTON, Bernard (1784-1849), 'the Woodbridge poet'. Barton worked in Alexander's Bank, Woodbridge, but longed to be a full-time poet. Southey admired his *Poetic Effusions.* Charles Lamb chided him for dwelling overmuch on his ailments. Edward Fitzgerald married Barton's daughter; not a happy partnership - Fitzgerald deliberately passing a Fat Lady Booth, saying 'I can see my own wife any hour'.

Barton is buried in the Friends' Meeting House grave-yard, **Woodbridge,** 'the most attractive small town in Suffolk (Shell Guide).

It was Canon Horace Wilkinson of Woodbridge who presented Cromwell's head to Sidney Sussex College, Cambridge. Also buried in Woodbridge is John Jarrold (1744-74), whose successors built up the publishing firm of the name. George Carlow, of the Bull Inn, insisted on being buried, not in the church, but in his stable.

Two rarities in Woodbridge: a 12th century tidal mill scheduled for restoration, and a steelyard for weighing wool, hay and hides at the Bell Inn, a machine unique in Suffolk and there are only a few others known in England.

BENNET, Henry, 1st earl of Arlington (1618-85), Lord Chamberlain. He returned from exile with Charles II and was suitably rewarded. A member of the Cabal, Arlington opposed Clarendon. He has been described as pompous, a flatterer and stupid, but had great taste and, said the diarist John Evelyn, 'was given to no expensive vice but building'. Evelyn found 'most laudable' the church Arlington built or reshaped in Euston Park. Charles II enjoyed visiting Euston, where Arlington retired after the failure of an attempt to impeach him.

Arlington buried **Euston.**

Church rebuilt late in 17th century, incorporating an earlier tower. Grinling Gibbons is credited with the panelling and the reredos. Memorial to the Dukes of Grafton. Arlington's daughter, aged 5, was married to Charles II's 9-year-old natural son, Henry Fitzroy, 1st duke of Grafton. Euston Station, London, got its name after the estate from being built on land owned by the Graftons.

⁺BLOOMFIELD, Robert (1766-1823), poet, author of *The Farmer's Boy.* Brought up by his widowed mother who kept a dame school. Robert worked in the fields at Sapriston from eleven years old until his health broke. He became a shoemaker in London, where he wrote of Giles, the farmer's boy, in the Suffolk countryside throughout the seasons. His work was published in 1800 with illustrations by Bewick and was much acclaimed for the accuracy and freshness of descriptions of the West Suffolk highlands. Bloomfield was briefly taken up by literary circles in London. However, fame's wheel soon turned and Bloomfield, his eyesight going, died poor in Bedfordshire.

Inscription to him in **Honington's** small church, which has a simple tower and a quaint stair turret.

*BOLEYN, Ann (1507-36). Yet another legend: that her heart was buried at **Erwarton,** opposite Harwich. In the 19th century a heart-shaped casket was indeed discovered in the chancel wall.

Massive towers characterise Erwarton church; inside much Tudor work, also considerably older monuments: Dewilliers family; Sir Bartholomew Bacon and wife Joan have a canopied tomb c.1400; Calthorpe tomb. A Calthorpe married Ann Boleyn's aunt, bolstering the story that the Queen's heart was removed by night after her execution and brought here. Erwarton's Tudor Hall has a turreted gateway.

BORROW, George [Henry] (1803–81), author and linguist. Very big, very strong, uncertain temper, brusque, yet sensitive: a solitary. His acknowledged father was a captain in the West Suffolk Regiment, but there was a persistent legend of a gypsy father, strengthened by George's appearance and preferences. His early years were spent following the regiment and it was officially then that he first met gypsies. Articled to solicitors, but studied languages, twelve of them by the age of 18; later he translated from 35. He abandoned law for literature, first writing for the Newgate Calendar. He wandered England, 1825–32, alone or with gypsies, a period of his life about which little is known: he may have visited southern Europe. He went to Russia for the British and Foreign Bible Society; then sent by the Society to Spain. Married a widow of means, older than himself, but lived alone, latterly at Oulton, where gypsies were always welcome. He briefly knew fame, then his work was adversely criticised, heightening his aloofness. Wrote *Lavengro, Romany Rye; The Bible in Spain;* and *Wild Wales.* His house near the Broads no longer exists.

Borrow said to be buried at **Oulton,** but his grave is at **West Brompton.**

The hovercraft was first tested by Christopher Cockerell at Oulton.

*BOUDICCA, Queen of the Iceni. Two more possible sites for her burial, both near the Norfolk border. One is the barrow on **Garboldisham Heath,** the second somewhere near St Andrew's Church, **Quidenham.**

BRITTEN, [Edward] Benjamin (1913-76), composer. 'If wind and water could write music, it would sound like Ben's' (attributed to Yehudi Menuhin). Britten's music, like that of Vaughan Williams in this respect, is often said to be quintessentially English, yet his friend and interpreter Rostropovich is said to have admired its 'Russianness'. Britten was a prolific composer of instrumental, vocal and choral works. During the War he lived for a time in the U.S.A., but was inspired to return to England after reading an article in *The Listener* by E M Forster on George Crabbe, and so came to Aldeburgh. The place, its atmosphere and its associations, particularly with Crabbe, loom large in Britten's work. The stage sets for his opera *Peter Grimes*, 1945, were based on the Tudor Moot Hall near the beach. In 1948 Britten founded the' Aldeburgh Festival with [Sir] Peter Pears and Eric Crozier. Imogen Holst, herself a musician, teacher and writer on music, worked devotedly as Britten's amanuensis. Britten was made a Companion of Honour 1953, given the Order of Merit 1965.
Buried **Aldeburgh** churchyard.

BROKE, Sir Philip Bowes Vere (1776-1841), sailor. Chiefly remembered for one action, 1813. Broke then commanded the frigate *Shannon* during the War with the United States. Patrolling off Boston, Massachusetts, he challenged the American frigate *Chesapeake* to come out and fight. The challenge was accepted: as soon as the ships had grappled, Broke led a boarding party and the *Chesapeake* was captured. His exploit gained him a baronetcy, but he was so severely wounded in the fighting that he had to retire. He lived in Broke Hall overlooking the Orwell estuary.
Buried **Nacton** church, like Admiral Vernon. Broke's brother, Sir Charles, was made quartermaster by Wellington during the Battle of Waterloo: he too has a memorial at Nacton.

CLARKSON, Thomas (1760-1846), abolitionist, 'duty's intrepid liegeman', according to Wordsworth's sonnet to him. From student days at Cambridge Clarkson dedicated himself to human liberty. He met William Wilberforce and Granville Sharpe and joined the committee, 1787, for suppressing the slave trade and speedily had the matter raised in Parliament. Clarkson sought witnesses to the horrors involved by visiting naval ships in many ports. He succeeded Wilberforce as leader of the abolitionists. He tried to gain the support of Russian Tsar. He helped found the Anti-Slavery Society. At last he knew triumph - as Wordsworth put it in his sonnet 'The bloodstained writing is for ever torn'. Clarkson went blind at 73, but his sight was restored by an operation. Made Freeman of the City of London, 1829.

Buried **Playford,** an obelisk marking his grave. Another monument to Clarkson in his birthplace, Wisbech.

COBBOLD (née Knipe), Mrs Elizabeth (1767-1824), writer. Original of Mrs Leo Hunter in the *Pickwick Papers*. She did write a lot, in prose, verse and drama. She ran 'Valentine Parties' about 1806 and later published sets as 'Cliff Valentines'. A worker for charity too.

A tablet to her, in praise of her 'benevolence and charity' in the civic church, St Mary Tower, **Ipswich.**

Her son, Rev. Richard Cobbold (1797-1877) was rector of Wortham from 1827. Also a writer - of verse inscriptions on headstones, parish history and, especially, a 'true narrative', Margaret Catchpole: a Suffolk Girl, a novel of smuggling and romantic adventure, based on fact, published in 1845 in three volumes, illustrated by the author. The real Margaret Catchpole was born in Nacton 1773, transported to Australia and died in Richmond, New South Wales.

CORDELL, Sir William (died 1581), Master of the Rolls. Solicitor General to Queen Mary, 1553. Prosecuted the poet-courtier Sir Thomas Wyat for high treason. Speaker of the Commons and Master of the Rolls. Interested in the Merchant Taylors' School, helped found St John's College, Oxford. He built Melford hall, its exterior remarkable for pepper-pot turrets and an octagonal gazebo. He entertained Elizabeth I sumptuously on her progress, 1578.

Holy Trinity, Long Melford

Monument in **Long Melford** church, with marble canopy and figures of various virtues.

The church is 'the first thing to see, not only in Melford, but in Suffolk' (Shell Guide). The Clopton family, who lived at the moated Tudor Kentwell Hall, Melford, have many windows and brasses and a chantry in the church. The large Lady Chapel was formerly used as a school (its wall bearing the multiplication table), a store and a coal cellar.

*CORDER, William (1804-28), murderer. His victim was Maria Marten at the Red Barn, Polstead, subject of a melodrama. Before his arrest Corder advertised for a wife, chose a schoolmistress from the 45 replies, and married her. The trial caused extraordinary interest; *The Times* gave it a quarter of its space. The rope used to hang Corder was sold at a guinea for an inch.

Skeleton in Suffolk General Hospital, **Bury St Edmunds**, where surgeon George Creed tanned Corder's skin for the cover of a history of the case. The book and a death mask (or his scalp) in Moyses Hall museum, Bury.

The Hall is a remarkable Norman house, thought to have belonged to a Jewish merchant. Bury is one of England's most delightful towns, with buildings of interest from medieval to modern times. Among them the remains of the Abbey, the 15th century Guildhall, the 17th century Town Hall remodelled by Robert Adam, town houses, shops and a fine Unitarian Chapel of 1711. Charles Dickens wrote of the Angel Hotel in Pickwick Papers. The Theatre Royal gave the world premiere of Charley's Aunt in 1892. 'The smallest pub in England', the Nutshell, is in the Traverse, near the Buttermarket. In 1214 the barons met at Bury and swore on the altar of the abbey church to force King John to sign the Magna Carta.

COWELL, Edward Byles (1826-1903), oriental scholar. The man who gave Edward Fitzgerald the Persian text of Omar Khayyam's *Rubaiyat*. Cowell was born in Ipswich and, in the public library when he was only 15, he picked up a book by Sir William Jones, which aroused his interest in Eastern literature. Though his father died the next year, Cowell got to Oxford as a

self-taught student and there he read Persian with Fitzgerald. Found the Omar manuscript during his six years
at Oxford. Cowell became Professor of History at the
newly-established Presidency College, Calcutta, 1856,
then president of the Sanskrit College. Professor of
Sanskrit at Cambridge, 1867. Published many Sanskrit
texts and translations.

Cowell was buried at **Bramford,** a church with an 18th
century leaded spire on a 14th century tower, where in
1644 the iconoclast Dowsing destroyed 841 'superstitious
pictures'.

*Dowsing left the church its 13th century piscina and
sedilia, chancel screen and Tudor cover to font.*

*CRABBE, George (1754-1832), poet. Crabbe was a
physically powerful man, of strong character and strong
passions, undeserving of Horace Smith's jibe of 'a Pope
in worsted stockings'. Life was difficult for Crabbe in
Aldeburgh and in London until, unexpectedly, Edmund
Burke, a stranger to him, became his patron, introducing him to Sir Joshua Reynolds and he to Dr
Johnson. Crabbe wrote *The Library* and *The Village* in
reaction from Goldsmith), but fame eluded him. He
took holy orders and wrote no more for 22 years. Then
he produced *The Parish Register*, 1807, and *The Borough* (Aldeburgh, no doubt), 1810. The spirit of East
Suffolk lives in Crabbe's verse.

There is a bust in St Paul's flint church overlooking
Aldeburgh and the sea. Crabbe's parents buried in the
churchyard.

CULLUM family.

Sir Thomas Cullum (1587?-1664), draper. He became
very wealthy as a London draper. Sheriff of London,
1646. He was a Royalist, for which he was penalised in
1647. Soon afterwards he retired and bought Hawsted
and Hardwick, near Bury St Edmunds. Cullum was made
a baronet at the Restoration, but somehow forfeited
royal favour.

He died at **Hawsted** and was buried there in a marble
tomb.

Windows in Hawsted church represent several members

of the family. Like Sir Thomas, his descendants turned to 'green thoughts in a green shade', many of them being garden-lovers.

Sir Dudley Cullum (1657-1720), horticulturist. Son of Sir Thomas. At Hawsted Sir Dudley introduced and culti-vated nearly all the exotics known to contemporary English gardeners. He was particularly keen on orange trees and had a greenhouse of unusual size. John Evelyn, the diarist, was a correspondent and gave him gardening advice. Cullum became the third baronet and, in 1690, High Sheriff.

His first wife died at Hawsted and was buried there. Sir Dudley married again and was buried at **Hawsted.** His widow remarried, but she too was buried at Hawsted in 1737.

Also buried at Hawsted was Rev John Cullum (1733-85), antiquary and divine. His father presented him to the rectory of Hawsted in 1762 and, in 1774, to the vicarage of Great Thurlow. He specialised in classics at Cambridge, then developed interests in antiquities, natural science and literature, not to mention botany. His wide knowledge made him well-known and his amiability made him well liked. He became sixth baronet. Cullum spent much of his life preparing *The History and Antiquities of Hawsted and Hardwick in the County of Suffolk,* in 1784. This work is said to have inspired Gilbert White's *Selbourne.* Cullum also collected material for a history of Suffolk.

Likewise buried at Hawsted was his brother, Sir Thomas Gery Cullum (1741-1831), surgeon. He trained as surgeon with William and John Hunter and practised at Bury St Edmunds very successfully. He was made Bath king-at-arms in 1771 (his second son succeeded him in 1800). He succeeded Sir John as seventh baronet. In 1813 he edited the second edition of his brothers History. He too loved botany, and the family's dedi-cation to its study was commemorated by the genus *Cullumnia* in the *Hortus Kewensis.*

DAY, John (1522-84), printer. Printed the first English edition of John Foxe's *Book of Martyrs* and took Foxe into his house. Day was one of the first to print music. The first English printer to use Saxon type (cut by

himself). The first person admitted to the livery when
the Company of Stationers was chartered by Philip and
Mary - but imprisoned under Mary. Master of the Company, 1580. A high reputation in Elizabeth's reign, so
easily obtained licences for printing; indeed, he volunt-
arily gave up 36 copyrights to benefit poor members of
the Stationers' Company. Married twice - 'each wyfe
twelve babes and each of them one more' [26 children].
Day buried at **Little Bradley** with wife, six sons and
five daughters. Brass to him with verse inscription
beginning 'Here lies the Daye that darkness could not
blind/ When Popish fogs had overcast the sun...' A
window to his memory, 1880, by the Stationers'
Company.
The little 11th century church has no aisle; the tower
perhaps as old as 10th century. Several other 16th
century brasses.

DE LE POLE family. Their associations and monuments
make **Wingfield** an epitome of late medieval English
history.
The first de la Pole commemorated in the former
collegiate church is Richard, who has a brass 1303.
Michael de la Pole, Earl of Suffolk, married the
daughter of Sir John Wingfield, head of the Black
Prince's Council, responsible for rebuilding Wingfield
church, 1362, and founding of Wingfield College. Wingfield has a canopy tomb with his helmet and armour
over it. Michael built the moated castle of 1382
(occupied to our day), which still has the original draw-
bridge and 14th century gatehouse.
His son, also Michael, 2nd earl, died at Harfleur, 1415,
under Henry V. Rare oak effigy of him and his wife
under his armour on tomb for which the church was
extended about 1470 at a cost of £75.8s.4d. by his son.
This William de la Pole, 4th earl and 1st duke of
Suffolk (1396-1450). His elder brother's death at
Agincourt narrated by Exeter in *Henry V;* his brother's
body boiled (quite customary) for ease in stripping
flesh, and bones brought to Wingfield. William was
immensely powerful under Henry VI, as Shakespeare's
play shows. Said to have been the lover of Margaret of

Anjou, whose marriage to Henry VI he arranged, but the terms he obtained were unpopular and, despite the suspiciously convenient death of his rival, Gloucester, in 1447, Suffolk was impeached and banished. Leaving England by ship he was trapped and beheaded at sea. Suffolk had fought in France with Bedford and Salisbury, but was defeated by Joan of Arc. He married Salisbury's widow, Alice, grand-daughter of Geoffrey Chaucer (her initials on one of the benches, the pride of the church, at **Fressingfield**).

William's son by Alice, John de la Pole, 2nd duke of Suffolk, chief steward of England at Edward IV's coronation, married Elizabeth of York, sister of Richard III and Edward IV. He and she have a joint tomb at Wingfield. John attacked and ransacked the Paston house at Hellesdon, 1465.

Wingfield church has a sentry-box shelter to protect the clergyman officiating at the graveside in bad weather.

DE VERE family, earls of Oxford. As mentioned in the Essex section, the table tombs of three earls of Oxford were moved from Earl's Colne in 1935. They were taken to **Bures St Mary.**

Here in the Chapel Barn on the site of a church, St Edmund was allegedly crowned on Christmas Day, 865. Above the village is a small thatched church, the Chapel of St Stephen, dedicated by Archbishop Stephen Langton as a private chapel to the manor of Tamy; some say it is on the site where Edmund was crowned. The Chapel (which is usually locked) was restored for the tombs.

Attributions: Robert de Vere, 5th earl, stone effigy c.1296, on tomb chest of c.1340. Thomas, 8th earl, 1371, alabaster tomb, with several niches on either side, each with two male weepers. Big alabaster tomb c.1417 for Richard, 11th earl, prominent at Agincourt, and his wife, Alice.

The church has a 14th century wooden porch, 15th century ceremonial font, and other monuments, including an early 14th century effigy of a knight, a member of the de Cornard family.

DOWSING, William (1596?-1675?), iconoclast. 'Parlia-mentary visitor for demolishing the superstitious pictures and ornaments of churches' in Suffolk, 1644. He demolished altars, removed candlesticks and defaced pictures and images. He visited 150 places in 50 days. Especially busy in and around Ipswich. Already at Clare in 1643 'we brake down 1000 Pictures superstitious: I brake down 200', he recorded. Also in 1643 wreaked 'godly thorough reformation' on University college chapels in Cambridge, not to mention destruction in the schools, 'Colledge Halls, Libraryes, and Chambers'. Unpunished at the Restoration.
Dowsing was born at **Laxfield** and is said to be buried there. Tablet to his memory, and his wife's tombstone. He 'visited' the church, where some pews were 'For Men Only', others 'For Women Only'.
Laxfield 16th century Guildhall turned into a museum.

*DRURY, Sir William (1527-79), marshal of Berwick. Much of his distinguished military service was in the north, where the northern earls rose in 1569. Drury raided Scotland, 1570, and, after many attempts to assassinate him, penetrated as far as Edinburgh in 1573. Sent to Ireland in 1576, he made a severe governor. Lord usher to the council in Ireland, 1578.
Drury died in Dublin but there is a bust in **Hawsted** church. The family is said to have given its name to Drury Lane, where they had a London house. Several other family monuments at Hawsted, Sir William's bust over the black sarcophagus of his son, Sir Robert (1617). Sir Robert's young daughters there too, Elizabeth and Dorothy. Elizabeth has an alabaster monument with a Latin inscription by John Donne, dean of St Paul's. Some say a box on the ear killed her at 15 and that she was loved by James I's son, Henry.
An earthquake, 1926, caused damage, now restored.

DULEEP SINGH, Maharajah (died 1893). A Sikh prince, he was proclaimed Maharajah at the age of five. During his reign the Koh-i-Nor diamond, which he possessed at the time, was brought to England in 1849: he followed some years later. Queen Victoria received him at

Windsor - he was very personable. He converted to Christianity in 1853, baptised with water from the Ganges. In 1863 he bought Elvenden Hall and set about refashioning the interior in the oriental style. The Maharajah gave the Ancient House, Thetford, as Breckland Museum. Passionately devoted to shooting, he once killed nearly 800 partridges in a day. Formerly on friendly terms with the Royal Family, he turned against them when his request for the return of the Koh-i-Nor was refused, calling the Queen 'Mrs Fagin... a receiver of stolen property'. He became dissatisfied with his grant of £198,000 from the British Government and his annual pension of £25,000; no doubt it was a come-down after personally owning 150 villages in Punjab and a salt-mine alone worth £45,000 a year. He was still able, however, to send a courier to Paris to buy caviar for him.

The Maharajah died in Paris, but was buried in **Elveden** churchyard, as was his wife, Bamba Muller, of Alexandria.

Elveden was later bought by the first Lord Iveagh, who created there what was the largest farm in England. He made further alterations to the house, 1899-1904, adding a white marble hall based on the Taj Mahal. The tower and cloisters were built in 1922 in memory of Lady Iveagh.

EDMUND, King and Saint (martyred 869). Until Edward III's time, Edmund was the patron saint of England; until Thomas Becket's cult, Edmund's shrine at Bury rivalled that of St James of Compostella. Edmund was King of the East Angles, 855, with his capital traditionally at Reedham [modern chain-ferry across the Yare]. Killed by Danes. His body taken to London, but ceremoniously returned to Boedericsworth (now **Bury St Edmunds**) in 1013. The magnificent Abbey still an impressive ruin.

Many legends. One tells that, fleeing the Battle of Thetford, Edmund was asked by a band of Danes where the king was and replied that he was in the fort [Framlingham] before he left, and was allowed to pass. Hoxne insists that Edmund was martyred there, after hiding under a bridge as a bridal party crossed, when the bride saw the gleam of his golden spurs in the water and betrayed his presence. **Hoxne** claims the site, marked by a marble cross, of the oak to which Edmund was tied for execution by Hingwar; he was beheaded after torture for refusing to renounce Christianity. The head called out and was discovered guarded by a wolf. Miracles happened at the chapel erected over it. When the body was removed to Bury, the head and body were found to be reunited and uncorrupted.

The Abbey itself is badly mutilated, but the west front of the abbey church still stands, as do two gatehouses and the 13th century abbot's bridge. The superb Norman tower in Churchgate Street was the ceremonial gateway for the abbey; it is now belfry for St James's, cathedral since 1914, the only one in Suffolk.

ELDRED, Sir John (1552-1632), traveller and merchant. In 1583 sailed for Aleppo, where Othello smote a Turk, in the *Tiger* (surviving a storm raised by the witches in *Macbeth*). Overland to the Euphrates and south along the river to Baghdad, city of the Thousand and One Nights, with 100 asses. Down the Tigris to Basra, Sindbad the Sailor's port. Left after six months with 70 barges, mainly spices, for Baghdad again. Back to Aleppo, with 4,000 camel loads. Three years, highly profitable, trading in Aleppo with perhaps the biggest covered suq (market) in the world, then home to England, extremely wealthy. Increased his fortune. Built 'Nutmeg Hall', named after the spice which helped make him rich (Hall burned down 1779). One of the first directors of the East India Company. Many other commercial interests.

A bust of Eldred over a brass skeleton in **Great Saxham** church, also brass showing him as an alderman of London.

Two windows in the church, 1816, have painted glass from France and Switzerland.

ELDRED, Thomas (died 1622), mariner. Perhaps a distant cousin of Sir John. Thomas is said to have sailed with Thomas Cavendish (1560-92), who came from

Trimley St Martin, near Harwich. Eldred may have been on both Cavendish's voyages, that of 1586 the more famous, since it circumnavigated the world. The second, 1591, was disastrous, and Cavendish died, his spirit broken, off Ascension Island. Eldred served some years from 1600 as factor or commander with the East India Company.

Buried, appropriately, at St Clement's, **Ipswich,** for it is near the quay and the sight of its wide low tower has gladdened generations of returning seamen. Sir Thomas Slade, who designed Nelson's *Victory,* also buried in St Clement's.

On the quay, the handsome Old Custom House, built in Victorian times in Palladian style.

St Clement's is one of a dozen medieval churches in Ipswich, the birthplace of Cardinal Wolsey. Only the gateway remains of the College of Regular Canons that Wolsey founded. The Royalist family, the Sparrowes, hid Charles II after the Battle of Worcester in their picturesque Ancient House. Gainsborough lived in the town and some of his paintings are in the collection, one of several, at Christchurch Mansion, a Tudor house altered in the 17th century, standing in its park. Mr Pickwick had an eventful visit to Ipswich, where misfortune befell him at the Great White Horse Inn. The Inn also put up George II in 1736, Nelson in 1800, and Louis XVIII of France in 1807.

*ELLIS, [Henry] Havelock (1859-1939), writer and authority on sex. Taught in New South Wales as a young man, returned to England and qualified in medicine, 1889, but turned to literature. Edited the Mermaid series of Old Dramatists from 1887. He wrote for monthly reviews and met early British socialists, such as Shaw, John Burns, H M Hyndman. Eleanor Marx, daughter of Karl, introduced Ellis to Olive Schreiner, author of *The Story of an African Farm,* with whom he had a passionate relationship until she returned to Cape Colony in 1889, and even then still kept in touch. Ellis's major work was the *Studies in the Psychology of Sex,* 1897-1928, which aroused a storm and were for long unpublishable in England - they could and did

appear in the U.S.A.
Ellis died **Hintlesham.**
The Elizabethan Hall, altered in the 18th century to current taste, was saved and restored in 1972 by Robert Carrier, who made it temporarily a centre, not only for gourmets, but for lovers of music and the arts.
Bronze bust of Ellis in **Ipswich** Museum.

FENN, Sir John (1739-94), antiquary. Born in Norwich and went to Caius College, Cambridge. Almost from the start his bent was antiquarian. He made his home at Dereham, Norfolk, in 1791 becoming Sheriff of the county. His main work was in editing the Paston letters, which he carried on with praiseworthy scholarship. In 1774 he bought many of the Paston letters from a Diss chemist (see Thomas Martin) and published the first two volumes in 1787, dedicating them to George III, who thereupon knighted him. The originals went to the Royal Library. Two more volumes followed in 1789.
Fenn was buried in the chancel of **Finningham** church, near Eye. Though much restored, it retains a medieval door in the south porch and medieval roof and font.
The fifth and last volume of the Paston letters was published by Fenn's nephew, William Frere, master of Downing College, Cambridge. All the manuscripts disappeared after Frere's death, prompting a suggestion that the letters were forged, but what happened was that some of the manuscripts had been overlooked for some years, while those in the Royal Library seem to have been borrowed and not returned by Dr Pretyman, Pitt's private secretary, and were discovered in the house of his descendants near Ipswich. Since 1933 the letters have been in the British Museum.

FITZGERALD, Edward (1809-83), poet and translator. Famous for his rendering of the *Rubaiyat* (quatrains) of Omar Khayyam, 1859. His orientalist friend, Cowell, discovered the manuscript in the Bodleian, Oxford, and gave it to Fitzgerald. Translation a failure until Rossetti and Swinburne happened to see copies in a penny box outside Quaritch's bookshop in St Martin's

Lane, London. Returning for more copies next day, they complained on finding the price raised to tuppence: soon it was a guinea. Not that Fitzgerald needed the money; he came from a wealthy family. Nor did he revel in his new fame. Fitzgerald also translated from Greek and Spanish. He lived in a cottage on his father's Boulge estate, later at Woodbridge. Eccentric, with a gift for friendship, ranging from Tennyson to uncomplicated young men. Disastrous marriage (see Barton). Fond of tobacco and a flask of wine. As a correspondent 'witty, picturesque and sympathetic' (Edmund Gosse).

Buried **Boulge.** The Victorian traveller, William Simpson, brought back seeds claimed to be from the rose over Omar's grave at Naishapur; they were raised at Kew Gardens and a rose was planted on Fitzgerald's grave in 1893. Six more roses sent from Naishapur in 1972 to mark the 2,500th year of Persian Empire.

GARDEN, Mrs John Lewis see Murat, Princess Caroline.

GARRETT, Richard III (1807-66), engineer. He enormously developed the already prominent firm specialising in agricultural machinery, established in Woodbridge, but moved to Leiston in 1778. Threshing machines and steam boilers were the speciality of the company, but they also developed a highly successful portable steam engine and made iron rick-stands, known as stringalls from their inventor, J Stringall of Ipswich. The firm was the first to drain Leiston marshes effectively.

There is a bust of Garrett in **Leiston-cum-Sizewell** church. The local Council put three of his stovepipe hats in a glass case in the Council Chamber.

The ruins of the abbey many but scattered, the most substantial being the 16th century gatehouse with turrets. After the Dissolution, corn was stored in the Lady Chapel, probably helping to keep it intact. Though the abbey is a Diocesan retreat it may sometimes be visited. Near the beach a hermit's cell of 1531 was fortified in 1940. Summerhill School, A S Neill's pioneering educational establishment, nearby. In 1958 Sizewell was chosen as the site of an atomic power station.

St Peter's, Yoxford

GRENFELL, William Henry, Baron Desborough (1855-1945), athlete, sportsman and public servant. A remarkable series of achievements, among them, oarsman at Oxford, twice swam Niagara pool below the falls, climbed Matterhorn by three different routes (and other Alpine peaks), also ascents in the Rocky Mountains. Deer-stalker, angler, big-game hunter. President of the MCC and of the Lawn Tennis Association. Local government service and various public duties, from president of the London Chamber of Commerce and president of the International Navigation Congress, London, 1923, to president of the Central Association of Volunteer Training Corps in the Great War.
Buried at **Little Bradley.**

*GREY, Lady Katherine (1541?-68), sister of Lady Jane Grey, grand-daughters of Henry VIII's sister, Mary Tudor. As Elizabeth I had no heirs, Katherine was next in succession. A maid of honour to Elizabeth, Katherine antagonised the queen by secretly marrying Edward Seymour, Lord Hertford, and bearing a son. Fearing a plot, Elizabeth sent Hertford and Katherine to the Tower, where in 1563 she had another son. That year plague broke out and Katherine was sent to her uncle at Pyrgo, Essex. After another spell in the Tower her health failed and she was moved by way of Ipswich and Snape to Cockfield Hall, Yoxford, near Minsmere, in the charge of Sir Owen Hopton. Katherine fell ill and died at Yoxford and seems to have been embalmed. At the funeral service at **Yoxford,** Hertford was not allowed to attend or to be represented. Katherine's body later taken to Salisbury Cathedral and buried beside Hertford's.
Yoxford is a charming village in 'the garden of Suffolk'. The church has a flint tower under a tall, slender, lead-covered spire, and the Cockfield Chapel. Cockfield Hall has been several times restored, once after a bomb in 1941: it has a fine columbarium. A few miles from Yoxford is the Westleton Heath nature reserve.

HENSLOW, Rev Professor John Stevens (1796-1861),

botanist. Recommended Charles Darwin, his favourite pupil, for the *Beagle;* took charge of the specimens sent home. He assisted Sir W J Hooker to form Kew Museum and popularised botany as professor at Cambridge. The rector of Hitcham from 1837 onwards. While staying at Felixstowe, Henslow recognised the value as fertiliser of deposits in Suffolk Cragg and named the nodules 'coprolites' - there is a Coprolite Street in Ipswich, the port for shipping fertilisers. At Hitcham, Henslow rendered many services to the parish, thitherto neglected, from schools (despite farmers' opposition), benefit clubs, cricket and athletic clubs to parish outings and 'lecturettes' at half-yearly flower shows. Active in founding the Ipswich Museum.

Buried **Hitcham;** a tablet in the choir, which is several steps up from the nave.

The church has splendid roofs in nave, chancel and choir.

HERVEY, Frederick, 4th earl of Bristol and bishop of Derry (1730-1803). His lavish tipping on his travels encouraged innkeepers in many continental towns to establish a Hotel Bristol. Extraordinary man; his eccentricities seem to justify the saying that there are men, women and Herveys. As well as a traveller, an earl and a bishop, Hervey was also a lawyer, art-lover and geologist - he discovered the geological formation of the Giants' Causeway. A reputation, too, as a gallant and interested in agriculture. Succeeding to the Hervey estates in 1779, he travelled and collected art treasures until about 1794 he began the extraordinary Ickworth Hall and estate: a park of 1,800 acres, eleven miles round. Vanbrugh planned the Hall. Hervey never saw the rotunda, 100 feet high, or any of the Hall, as he left for Italy and died while abroad. His body brought back to **Ickworth.** Memorials to the Earls of Bristol in the 13th century church.

Most of the Hall acquired by the National Trust from the Hervey family in 1956. Its art treasures are exemplarily displayed. In the park, landscaped by Capability Brown, the little River Linnet rises, a tributary of the Lark.

HOWARD family.

Thomas II, Earl of Surrey and 3rd duke of Norfolk (of the Howard house) (1473-1554). Opposed Wolsey and gained from the Dissolution. He presided at the trial of Ann Boleyn, his niece. He suppressed the Pilgrimage of Grace, 1536. He opposed Thomas Cromwell and arrested him. His dangerous rival, the Earl of Hertford, had the duke's son, Henry (see below) executed for high treason and the duke himself arrested, but Henry VIII died the night before the execution and Mary released Howard. The duke sought favour by bringing the body of his son's companion, the Duke of Richmond, from Thetford Priory to Framlingham.

Thomas II buried in the church of St Michael, **Framlingham,** in a great white tomb, with his second wife Elizabeth Stafford, 1558; the alabaster tomb, carved and painted 'bears comparison with anything in northern Europe' (Shell Guide).

Henry, Earl of Surrey (1517-47), poet, soldier and courtier. Son of the above. Surrey's attainments led later to a comparison with Sir Philip Sidney. High in Henry VIII's favour at first, boyhood companion of Henry Fitzroy, Duke of Richmond (1519-36), Henry's illegitimate son. Surrey wrote the first English blank verse and was the first to use sonnet form, though not the rhyme scheme of his master, Petrarch. Distinguished in the field at Montreuil, near Boulogne, 1541. He lost all, including his life, through the power struggle with Edward Seymour, Earl of Hertford (later Duke of Somerset). Surrey was quite unable to match the advantage of Jane Seymour's having given Henry VIII his only legitimate son. Surrey was executed on very flimsy charges. His body was removed by his son to **Framlingham;** discovered in 1835 under his effigy.

Other Howard tombs. Also the tomb (restrained in comparison) of Sir Robert Hitcham (1636), who bought castle, park and lodges, bequeathing them to his college, Pembroke, Cambridge.

The church has a famous organ of 1674, made for Pembroke College. Framlingham is much admired, its castle with a dozen towers and the curtain wall rising from the town. Mary came to Framlingham from

Norfolk to be proclaimed Queen 1553; here she had Bishop Ridley arrested.

HYAM, Mrs Elizabeth (died 1738). Widowed four times. She was in her 113th year when she was 'hastened to her death' by a fall.
A tablet in **Boxford** church, which has a unique wooden porch.
The west tower has a little spire. Also in the church a delightful brass, 1606, to the rector's infant son, David Birde, asleep in a little cot.

IVES, John (1751-76), antiquary. A short, but brilliant life. Elected Fellow of the Society of Antiquaries in 1771 and a Fellow of the Royal Society the next year. Inspired to antiquarian studies by 'Honest Tom' Martin. Collected antiquities, manuscripts, coins, medals and old paintings. He had a private press and published papers written by himself and others on local antiquities and various other subjects. Appointed an Honorary Member of the College of Arms, 1774, by the efforts of the Earl of Suffolk and the title of Suffolk Herald Extraordinary was revived for him.
Buried **Belton,** Yarmouth, with his father and grandfather.

KEPPEL, Augustus, 1st Viscount Keppel (1725-86), admiral. Very long, very active service in the navy, which he entered when only 10 years old. With Anson round the world. He arranged a treaty with the Bey of Algiers at a stormy meeting in 1748. He tried to save Admiral Byng from execution. Keppel received vast prize money, a source of envy, from taking Havana in 1762. Pro-Rockingham, he was involved in party intrigues, but continued in command. He found that Lord Sandwich had so neglected and run down the navy that he had to retire to Spithead. Keppel scraped together a fleet and met the French off Ushant in 1779, but his second in command, Sir Hugh Palliser, failed to back him, forcing another retirement. Both admirals were court-martialled and both acquitted. Keppel became a hero and there were anti-government demonstrations. He left the sea and served under Rockingham, but his health had been broken at Havana. A wall monument to Keppel in **Elveden** church, much rebuilt since the 13th century.

KIRBY, John (1670-1753), topographer. Surprisingly little is known about the man who first made so much known about Suffolk. He was a schoolmaster at Orford and later had a mill at Wickham Market. For three years, 1732-5, he scoured the county, collecting material for *The Suffolk Traveller*, published 1735. He was interested in antiquities and wrote of them, as well as giving particulars about places. There were many subsequent editions of the *Traveller*, reprints and additions, some in Kirby's lifetime. In 1736 he issued 'A Map of the County of Suffolk', illustrated with views and coats of arms. His sons, John Joshua (a great friend of Gainsborough) and William, published an improved edition.
Kirby buried in the churchyard of St Mary Tower, **Ipswich.**
The fact that Ipswich Museum devotes practically all its space to Suffolk material would surely have pleased Kirby.

KYTSON, Sir Thomas (1485-1540), cloth merchant and sheriff of London, 1533. A member of the Merchant Adventurers' Company. Master of the Mercers' Company. Very wealthy, not only from cloth, but also from dealing in 'wool, Venese gynger, sugar, copper, cornish tyn', furs, pepper, cloves and madder. John Wilbye was the family musician at Hengrave, the magnificent white-brick, embattled house, built 1525-35, its gatehouse twin-turretted. Here Elizabeth I, Leicester and the whole court were entertained on a lavish scale in 1578. Kytson married John Bourchier's widow, Margaret, Countess of Bath.
Buried, with much state, at **Hengrave.** Monuments to Sir Thomas and his two wives - this an enormous marble and alabaster tomb - and to Bourchier. An alabaster monument to Lord Darcy and other monuments to the Gage family (Sir William Gage (1657-1727), said to

have introduced the greengage from France, it taking its English name from him).

LOTT, William (Willy) (died 1849). He of Willy Lott's Cottage on the millstream near Flatford Mill, the subject of Constable's painting *The Hay Wain*. Willy owned Valley Farm, being born there, and Constable's biographer, Leslie, says that 'he passed more than 80 years without spending four whole days away from it'. Buried **East Bergholt,** Constable's birthplace.
The church tower begun by Wolsey, they say, but never finished. The bells are hung in a 16th century wooden frame in the churchyard; they are not pulled, but pushed, being counterweighted. Randolph Churchill lived not far away at Stour.

LYDGATE, John (1370?-1451?), poet. Born at Lidgate, hence his surname. His boyhood and most of his life spent at Bury St Edmunds Abbey. He wrote lengthily about declines and falls, e.g. Troy, Thebes, princes, but had a mischievous side to his nature, shown in his shorter works and in revelations of boyhood truancies and raids on abbey orchards and vines. He complained of poverty, often and without much justification, for he was regularly rewarded. Associated with Caxton, he revered Chaucer (continuing the *Canterbury Tales* and sending his manuscripts for criticism). He provided verse on official occasions and was the chief court poet after Gower died in 1408.
Lydgate 'doubtless buried in the **Bury** monastery'*(D.N.B.)*
By the heyday of the Abbey the monks had collected such relics as parings of St Edmund's nails, the coals on which St Lawrence was roasted, St Thomas's boots and enough pieces of the Holy Cross to make a complete cross.
Portrait brass (restored) of the poet in **Lidgate** church, built on the site of the vanished castle.

MACRO, Cox (1683-1767), antiquary. Father a .wealthy grocer, alderman and several times chief magistrate of Bury St Edmunds; built Cupola House, one of Bury's best buildings; married Miss Cox, hence son's unusual

first name. After Cambridge, Cox Macro went to Leyden University. Appointed chaplain to George II, but, being rich, sought no further preferment. A linguist, he collected paintings, coins and medals, building up a large library of rare books and manuscripts, especially poetry. He modernised Little Haugh Hall, Norton, and had it decorated by well-paid continental artists.
Buried **Norton.**
Eight outstanding misericords in the church, including the martydom of Saints Edmund and Andrew. Font has a wodewose (wild man of the woods).

MARTEN, Maria (1804?-28), murdered in the Red Barn, Polstead, by William Corder. Their infant son died in infancy. Corder promised to marry Maria if she left home. After she had departed, lack of news worried her stepmother, who dreamed of the Red Barn murder. Maria's body was found, Corder arrested at Brentford, Middlesex, convicted and hanged at Bury St Edmunds. The Red Barn has burned down.
Maria is buried in St Mary's churchyard, **Polstead.**
The church, standing alone, incorporates Roman bricks and has a stone spire, said to be unique in Suffolk. Polstead's Gospel Oak is claimed to be 1,000 years old.

MARTIN, Thomas (1697-1771), antiquary. Although he liked to be known as 'Honest Tom Martin', he was not always scrupulous in handling material he collected. A lawyer, but he neglected his practice. He inspired John Ives. He collected details for a history of Thetford and left notes on 200 Suffolk churches (bought by Sir John Cullum). For a long time Martin was senior Fellow of the Society of Antiquaries. His lack of money sense led to his impoverishment and he had to sell many of his books and some of his manuscript collection, including many unpublished Paston letters sold years previously by the 2nd earl of Yarmouth, last of the Pastons, to a Norfolk antiquary, Peter Le Neve. Martin married Le Neve's widow, thus acquiring the letters. From Martin's library the letters went to Thomas Worth, a chemist, of Diss. They were next bought by John Fenn (q.v.) for publication.
Buried at **Palgrave** with other members of his family:

commemorated in the carved porch, 1771, by Sir John Fenn.
The authoress Mrs Anna Laetitia Barbauld, having married Rev. Rochemont Barbauld, 1774, established a boys' boarding school in Palgrave and ran it until 1785.

MURAT, Princess Caroline Letitia (Mrs John Lewis Garden) (1833-1902). It is strange to find the tomb of Napoleon Bonaparte's great-niece in Suffolk. The Princess was the grand-daughter of Joachim Murat (1767-1815), son of an innkeeper, who rose to be marshal of France and King of Naples, for long one of Napoleon's most capable and loyal supporters, even after Waterloo fighting to keep Naples, but was captured and shot. Murat married Napoleon's youngest sister, Caroline. The Princess, luckier in life than many members of her family, married a French baron (Charles Chafiron, some say), was widowed, then met and married John Lewis Garden, of Redisham Hall. That was how she came to live out her life in Suffolk. After his downfall King Louis Philippe came to England, as did Napoleon III and his Empress Eugenie, so Princess Murat had precedents.
Buried in a tomb erected, it seems, by her three children, bearing a crown and fleur-de-lys, outside **Ringsfield** church, which is thatched.
It is remarkable for having a rare Elizabethan exterior brass to Nicholas Garnys, High Sheriff of Suffolk, his wife and eleven children, above a mermaid. Inside is rich Jacobean woodwork. On the wall a monument in black and red to Robert Selford, rector. He put it up himself while he was alive - but someone else had to add the date, 1701.
Not far away, Barsham was the birthplace of Catherine Suckling, Nelson's mother, a descendant of John Suckling, the Cavalier poet and, according to Aubrey, inventor of cribbage.

MURRELL, James (1812?-60), white witch. Born in Hadleigh, seventh son of a seventh son, known as 'Cunning' Murrell, made a good living as a white magician. He claimed an ability to exorcise spirits and overcome witchcraft by counter-spells. He equipped himself with a magic mirror for locating lost or stolen property, a telescope for looking through walls and a copper amulet which could distinguish honest from dishonest clients. It is said that clients diagnosed by Murrell as bewitched gave him samples of their hair, nails, blood and urine, which he put into his iron 'witch -bottles'. He heated the mixture to boiling at midnight, maintaining strict silence, to provoke burning pains in the witch's body, thus causing her (less often him) to revoke the spell. Once he was brought a girl barking like a dog, after being cursed by a gypsy woman; when the witch-bottle was heated it exploded and the next day the charred body of a woman was found in a nearby country lane. Murrell was secretive, moving about only at night, carrying an umbrella whatever the weather. He predicted the exact time of his death the day before he died.

Buried in **Hadleigh** churchyard in an unmarked grave.

Other 19th century white witches reported from East Anglia include the Ipswich man known as 'Old Winter' and Old Mother Jenkins, the Goose Charmer of Epping Forest. Less benevolent was Jabez Few, of Willingham, Cambridgeshire, who had white mice as his imps; he lived on until the 1920s.

NORTH, Sir Dudley (1641-91), financier and economist. When a child a beggar woman stole him for his clothes, but he was soon rescued. Tall and vigorous, very strong. He spent 1662-80 as a merchant in Smyrna, being very influential in Constantinople. A remarkable linguist, especially in Turkish. He made his own way by ability and force of character. Sheriff of London, 1682. Commissioner for Customs, then at Treasury, He advocated free trade. He avoided trouble under James II and William III, although a very staunch Jacobite and suspected (the charge dropped) of packing juries who condemned Algernon Sidney and other Whigs in 1682.

North was buried at Covent Garden Church, but his body was removed to **Little Glemham,** where he has a white marble monument.

The church has brass inscriptions to the Glemham family, who acquired the place in the 16th century and built the Hall.

Newbourne Church

NORTH, Dudley Long (1748-1828), politician. A nice man - he gave money, of which he had a lot, to George Crabbe. A loyal Whig, MP for 40 years. Lost one election by 10 votes to 6; won another by 5 to 3. Why elect him, when he had a severe speech defect and couldn't speak in the Commons? Because he gave celebrated political dinners to Whigs; he was a good organiser, for instance of the trial of Warren Hastings; an important associate of Fox. Boswell credited him with acuteness of wit; an example, when requested by Edward Gibbon to repeat praise by Sheridan, North answered, "Oh, he said something about your voluminous pages." Through Mrs Thrale, North met Dr Johnson, who considered him 'a man of genteel appearance, and that is all'. North was a mourner at Sir Joshua Reynold's funeral and a pall-bearer at the funeral of Edmund Burke.

Buried at **Little Glemham.** The monument showing him seated was sculpted in Italy.

PAGE, George (died 1870), the Suffolk Giant. He stood 7ft 7 in. in his stockinged feet. He was exhibited in many towns in England. He married a very short woman. His brother Meadows was also a 'giant'.

Buried at **Newbourne** beside the church path.

The church has a flint tower porch, with pinnacles and battlements, brick body, hammerbeam roof and 15th century font. The medieval Hall with lofty Elizabethan extensions is described as wonderfully unspoilt.

*RAEDWALD (died c.624), King of East Anglia from c.599. Supposed by some to be commemorated in the great ship burial at **Sutton Hoo.** St Etheldreda was of his family. Raedwald came of the Uffinga dynasty founded c.550 by Wuffa, of Swedish extraction. Raedwald greatly extended his kingdom. His wife was pagan and, as well as an altar to Christ, he erected another for those who worshipped devils.

The site of Sutton Hoo comprises many mounds above the River Deben; some excavated in 1938 under the direction of the gifted local archaeologist, Basil Brown. One revealed the boat, over 80 feet long, for 38 oars-

*men, which had been dragged up from the river one
hundred feet below to the sandy, bracken-covered hill-
side. 1,000 tons of soil covered the ship. It is now
established that there was a body buried there. The
date of burial is fixed to the first quarter of the 7th
century by coins and silver plate with marks of a
Byzantine emperor. The owner of the estate, Mrs Edith
M Pretty, generously gave the finds to the British
Museum (replicas in Ipswich Museum). They are of
almost incalculable interest, the first and richest find
of the burial of an East Anglian aristocrat or ruler.
Loaded into a cabin admidships were weapons, armour,
helmet, shield, sceptre, magnificent gold buckle, a purse
with gold hinges containing 40 gold coins from Gaul,
harp ornaments, utensils and much else, even a pillow
stuffed with goose down.*

*The whole site is being systematically excavated. It is
now known to go back to Neolithic times. Other Anglo-
Saxon boats may await discovery.*

RANSOME, Robert (1795-1864), ironfounder (agricultural machinery maker). Of the Quaker family that
established a brass and iron foundry in Norwich, but
moved to the Orwell Works, Ipswich, in 1789 with £200
capital. By 1850 the firm had over 1,500 workers,
thanks to a series of innovations, and it has continued
to expand (under modified names). Among its early
achievements: Stoke Bridge, the first iron bridge at
Ipswich 1819; in 1803 'the most important invention
ever made in connection with ploughs', immediately
adopted, never superseded - a share that, thanks to the
casting process, maintained a sharp cutting edge; the
first lawn-mower 1832 and, the same year, the first
self-moving steam engine; 1844 the renowned YL
plough; 1850-60 development of John Fowler's world-
famous steam plough.

Ransome died during his only extended pleasure trip, a
continental tour, at St Goar on the Rhine. He was
buried in unconsecrated ground in **Ipswich** Cemetery,
Section V, Division 10, Grave 4.

SAMSON (1135-1211), Abbot of Bury St Edmunds. Very

able, very energetic. His chaplain Jocelin of Brakelonde, whose *Cronica* inspired Thomas Carlyle's *Past and Present*, describes Samson: medium height, losing hair (but eyebrows sometimes shaved), prominent nose, keen eyes, acute sense of hearing. Samson was a friend of Richard I. He freed the abbey of debt, and pushed through economic reforms unpopular with the monks, who disliked, too, his encouragement of the town's struggle for liberty. Various restorations and additions to the abbey church under Samson's rule (e.g. bell tower at the west end). He made a deer park and allowed his guests to hunt, but Jocelin says he never touched venison.

Buried in the Chapter House, **Bury.**

SIMON OF SUDBURY (executed 1381), Archbishop of Canterbury. Son of a Sudbury clothier, educated in law at the University of Paris. The Pope sent him to England as chancellor of Salisbury. Later Bishop of London, then appointed, 1375, to Canterbury. He crowned Richard II. Lord Chancellor in 1379. Learned and eloquent, but pliable. He sympathised with John Wyclif, but proceeded against him and had it on his conscience until death. He imprisoned John Ball. He agreed to apply the hated Poll Tax, which brought on the Peasants' Revolt. He was captured by Wat Tyler's men and clumsily beheaded on Tower Hill.

His body was given a luxurious tomb in Canterbury Cathedral. His head, which had been exposed on London Bridge, was taken to St Gregory's Church, **Sudbury,** and his skull is still there in a glass case.

There is a table tomb in St Gregory's for Thomas Carter (died 1700), with a Latin inscription relating 'a wondrous thing', that on the day he died 'a Sudbury Camel passed through the eye of a needle, if thou hast wealth, go and do likewise. Farewell'.

An old clothing and market town on the Stour and Gainsborough's birthplace, Sudbury refuses to accept that it was the original of Eatanswill in The Pickwick Papers.

SPRING, Thomas III (died 1523), clothier. Very wealthy: his widow was assessed at £1,000 in goods, and his son joined the landed gentry. **Lavenham** owes much to Thomas Spring, notably the campanile, for which he left £200. There is a Spring Chapel in the church, but of the Spring brasses only that to Thomas's father remains.

Lavenham is generally characterised as delightful, an old wool town having many half-timbered houses, a Wool Hall and a timber-framed Guildhall. At Shilling Old Grange Jane Taylor looked through an oriel window at a sight which prompted her 'Twinkle, twinkle, little star'. Old market cross preserved, as is a 1725 hand-operated fire engine.

TAYLOR, Dr Rowland (1509-60), Protestant martyr. Greatly loved in Hadleigh, where he was rector. This giant of a man openly defied Mary I's Roman Catholic policy and was repeatedly tried in London, but remained obdurate. When Bishop Bonner was about to degrade Taylor by a blow from his crozier, he was warned not to, or he in turn would be struck, with dire consequences. Taylor agreed that he would have fought back 'in my master's quarrel'. He was returned to Hadleigh for execution and a public demonstration supported him, hindering the sheriff and his minions for a time. Taylor died on **Aldham Common,** the first Suffolk martyr of 18 men and women. A stone monument marks the place.

In Hadleigh church (remarkable furnishings) a brass, one of many, is a palimpsest, showing Dean Hadleigh on one side and, on the other, part of the continental brass from which it was cut. Hadleigh 'rivals any Cotswold town' (Shell Guide). A fine medieval bridge over the Stour, a 15th century timber-framed Guildhall with two overhanging storeys, red-brick towers of Deanery near the 14th century flint and freestone church with its tapering lead-covered spire.

TUDOR, Mary (1496-1533), Queen of France, sister of Henry VIII. Betrothed in 1507 to Charles, prince of Castile, afterwards Emperor Charles V, but the match called off. She married Louis XII of France and was crowned Queen on the 5th November, 1514; on 1st

January, 1515, Louis died. To the displeasure of Henry VIII, Mary married his former friend Charles Brandon, Duke of Suffolk, 1515, Henry insisting on financial recompense for agreeing. Mary liked Catherine of Aragon and hated Ann Boleyn. Mary's daughter, Frances, by Charles Brandon had two daughters, Lady Jane and Lady Katherine Grey.

Mary buried in **Bury St Edmunds** Abbey, reinterred in St Mary's Church on the Dissolution. Her coffin was opened in 1784 and Horace Walpole and others obtained locks of her hair.

15th century St Mary's, across from the Cathedral, is famous for the roofs of its nave and chancel. In the north aisle there is a chapel to the Suffolk Regiment, which has its own museum in the town.

Bury has a memorial fountain to Ouida (Marie Louise Ramee) a French teacher's daughter, born here; she lived mostly in Italy, dying poor despite many novels much admired at the end of the 19th century.

VERNON, Edward (1684-1757), admiral. Popular in his lifetime for the capture with very few casualties of Porto Bello, 1739, not as spectacular as then thought, for it was defenceless. Less popular in the navy because he diluted the men's rum ration; they called him Old Grog, originally because he customarily wore an old grogram cloak (or trousers, some say). He took to railing against the Admiralty in letters and pamphlets and he was finally cashiered. MP for Ipswich for the last 16 years of his life.

Lived at **Nacton,** where he was buried.

Vernon's house, Orwell Park, was rebuilt in the year of his death and again in 1854, this time by Col. George Tomline, MP, who did so much to develop Felixstowe.

WARD, Samuel (1577-1640), Puritan divine. A redoubtable figure as a preacher and also as a gifted caricaturist. The town preacher of Ipswich (at St Mary Tower) 1603-35; also preached in Cambridge and London. Ward was briefly imprisoned for a caricature of the Spanish ambassador. Accused of non-conformity by Bishop Harsnett, 1622. The next year Ipswich corporation

declined James I's personal request to suspend Ward. Later he displeased Laud. He counselled young Suffolk Puritans to emigrate to America, but said that older people should stay and resist (600 Suffolk Puritans settled a Massachusetts Ipswich in 1633). Ward at last dismissed and imprisoned. He fled to Holland on his release, but returned and bought for £140 the house provided for him by Ipswich in 1610.
Buried at St Mary Tower, **Ipswich.** Inscription: 'Watch Ward! yet a little while/And He that shall come, will come'.
St Mary Tower was disastrously rebuilt in Victorian Gothic.

WINTHROP, Adam (1548?-1623), wealthy clothier, Lord of the manor of Groton, father of John Winthrop of New England.Adam is buried in the family grave, – **Groton;** so too his father and John's first two wives.
The flint church has lovely flowing tracery in the east window; glass put in by Winthrop descendants, 1875. In U.S.A. Groton is a famous school.

YOUNG, Arthur (1741-1820), agriculturalist and writer. Precocious in love and literature, he began a history of England while still at school. He failed in journalism, so turned farmer and failed again. Then he used his farming to good account in books and pamphlets and his monthly 'Annals of Agriculture', 46 volumes, much of them written by himself, but also contributions from Priestley, Jeremy Bentham, Coke of Holkham, 'Turnip' Townshend and by 'Ralph Robinson of Windsor', otherwise George III. Young toured England, Wales and Ireland, surveying agriculture; he advocated enclosures and large farms. *Travels in France* (1787-90) show the coming of the Revolution and its effects. Like his work on English agriculture, the *Travels* are most informative, highly interesting and well written. His fame extended through France to Russia and the United States. Young was very depressed by the death of his beloved daughter Martha Ann ('Bobbin') at 14 in 1797, but continued to work at the Board of Agriculture, to which Pitt had appointed him in 1793. Young was blir from 1811. He was visited by his relative, Fanny Burney, who described his home in her novel *Camilla*. Young buried at **Bradfield Combust,** where his father, the rector, planted avenues of lime trees.

The Church has a wall painting c.1390 of St George as a crusader to commemorate a lord of the manor who died crusading.

St Peter & St Paul's, Hoxne [see page 127]

My best thanks for information generously offered by Mr M F Ingham of the Institute of Astronomy, University of Cambridge; Mr George D Kissell of Buckhurst Hill, Essex; and Mrs O E Wright of Whittlesea, Essex.

Until a few years ago libraries would have been entitled to special thanks for the reference and other services they provide: no longer – through no fault of theirs, enforced cuts in funds have severely reduced the extent to which they can help. All the same it is a pleasure to record that the Local Studies Service of Essex, Norfolk and Suffolk County Libraries did far more than could have reasonably been expected, as did Reigate Library Information Service and the library of the East Surrey College. In addition to the *Dictionary of National Biography* and other standard reference works, the reader in search of further information will find, as I did, much of interest in the following:

Betjeman, John, editor. Collins' Guide to English parish churches. 1958.

Greenwood, Douglas. Who's buried where in England. Constable, 1982.

Mee, Arthur. Relevant volumes in the King's England series. Hodder & Stoughton.

Pevsner, Nicholas. Relevant volumes in the Buildings of England series. Penguin.

Nuggets of information are to be gathered from such sources as road books published by the Automobile Association and *Folklore, Myths and Legends of Britain* (Readers' Digest).

More specifically:

Cambridgeshire

Benstead, C R. Portrait of Cambridge. Hale, 1974.

Jennett, Sean. Travellers' guide to Cambridgeshire and the Isle of Ely. Darton, Longman & Todd, 1972.

Manning, S A. Portrait of Cambridgeshire. Hale, 1978.

Scarfe, Norman. Shell guide to Cambridgeshire. Faber, 1983.

Essex
Addison, William. Portrait of Epping Forest. Hale, 1977.
    Essex worthies. Phillimore, 1973.
Crouch, Marcus. Essex. Batsford, 1969.
Jarvis, Stan. Essex pride. Ian Henry, 1984.
    View into Essex. Terence Dalton, 1979.
Morgan, Glyn. The romance of Essex inns. Ian Henry, 1983.
Salmon, John. The Suffolk-Essex border. Boydell Press, 1977.
Scarfe, Norman. Shell guide to Essex. Faber, 1968.
Norfolk
Dorman, Bernard E. Norfolk. Batsford, 1972.
Harrod, Wilhelmina. Shell guide to Norfolk. Faber, 1982.
Manning, S A. Portrait of Broadland. Hale, 1980.
Wallace, Doreen, and R P Bagnall-Oakeley. Norfolk. Hale, 1951.
Suffolk
Burke, John. Suffolk. Batsford, 1971.
Jobson, Allan. North-east Suffolk. Coldharbour, 1948.
    Suffolk hours. Hale, 1979.
    Suffolk villages. Hale, 1971.
Scarfe, Norman. Shell guide to Suffolk. Faber, 1976.
    Suffolk landscape. Hodder & Stoughton, 1972.
Wilson, Derek. A short history of Suffolk. Batsford, 1977.

GEOGRAPHICAL INDEX

NAME INDEX

St Mary's, Polstead [see page 138]